# Marilyn Manson
## THE UNAUTHORIZED BIOGRAPHY

Copyright © 1997 Omnibus Press
(A Division of Book Sales Limited)

Written by Kalen Rogers
Cover & Book designed by EMA

US ISBN 0.8256.1643.3
UK ISBN 0.7119.6754.7
Order No. OP 48034

All rights reserved. No part of this book may be reproduced in any form or by any electronic or mechanical means, including information storage or retrieval systems, without permission in writing from the publisher, except by a reviewer who may quote brief passages.

Exclusive distributors:
BOOK SALES LIMITED
8/9 Frith Street, London
W1V 5TZ, UK.

MUSIC SALES CORPORATION
257 Park Avenue South,
New York, NY 10010, USA.

MUSIC SALES PTY LTD.
120 Rothschild Avenue,
Rosebery, NSW 2018,
Australia.

*To the Music Trade only:*
MUSIC SALES LIMITED
8/9 Frith Street,
London W1V 5TZ, UK.

Photo Credits:
Lili Wilde/All Action/Retna:1, 6, 7, 29, 31, 56, 57; Rodolphe Baras/LFI: 3,18, 49, 51, 67, 77; Joe Hughes/LFI: 4, 5, 27; Redferns/Retna: 8, 10, 15, 20, 21, 36, 46; Gary Malerba/Corbis: 11,16, 44, 45; M. Gerber/Corbis: 13; Kristin Callahan/LFI: 22; Frank Forcino/LFI: 25, 32, 74, 79; Justin Thomas/All Action/Retna: 26, 55, 61; Ilpo Musto/LFI: 30; Milkman: 33, 75; Suzanne Moore/All Action/Retna: 39, 54; Sin/Tony Mott/Corbis: 40, 58; Kelly A. Swift/Retna: 42, 43, 48, 68; Stills/Retna: 52, 53, 59; Kevin Mazur/LFI: 65; Sam Hain/LFI: 66; Dana Frank/Corbis: 69; John Galdwin/All Action/Retna: 70, 71; Tibor Bozi/Corbis: 80

Front cover photograph:
Tibor Bozi/Corbis
Back cover: Redferns/Retna

Printed in the United States of America by Vicks Lithograph and Printing Corp.

# WHAT in GOD'S NAME is GOING ON?

A troupe of what appear to be escapees from the Victoria's Secret chapter of the local insane asylum have taken the nineties music scene by the throat and don't seem prepared to let go until they've converted every last one of America's youngsters and whipped the moral majority into such a frenzy they'll be late to church. The band that call themselves Marilyn Manson has caused an uproar with their album *Antichrist Superstar* and accompanying "Dead to the World" tour unlike anything seen in recent years.

Their frontman, the Reverend Manson, namedrops to the tune of Nietzsche, Darwin, and Milton in conversation and says things like "the juxtaposition of diametrically opposed archetypes" when asked what Marilyn Manson means. Hey, he might not be the best-looking guy on MTV, but he may well rank among the most intelligent. As *New York* magazine put it, "For a guy with a woman's name who likes to perform in a G-string and hernia truss, singer Manson gets a tremendous amount of respect." He may scare the hell out of some people, but his core ethic is actually pretty right-on: "The trick is to enjoy each and every day and squeeze every ounce that you can out of it - that is the true Marilyn Manson attitude." Well, a bit of *carpe diem*, a splash of Satanism, a few nights in jail, and a mad, magical brand of music may not be everyone's cup of tea, but it has served this "dirty, dirty rock star" quite well.

From the swamplands of Southern Florida they came, a whacked-out little outfit called Marilyn Manson and the Spooky Kids. Feeding themselves on nursery rhymes and magic tricks, they grew and grew until they were big enough to leave the death-metal scene of their youth and head to the candyland of MTV and record deals. Their fearless leader had hatched a fiendish plot, and the beautiful people weren't watching their backs. . . .

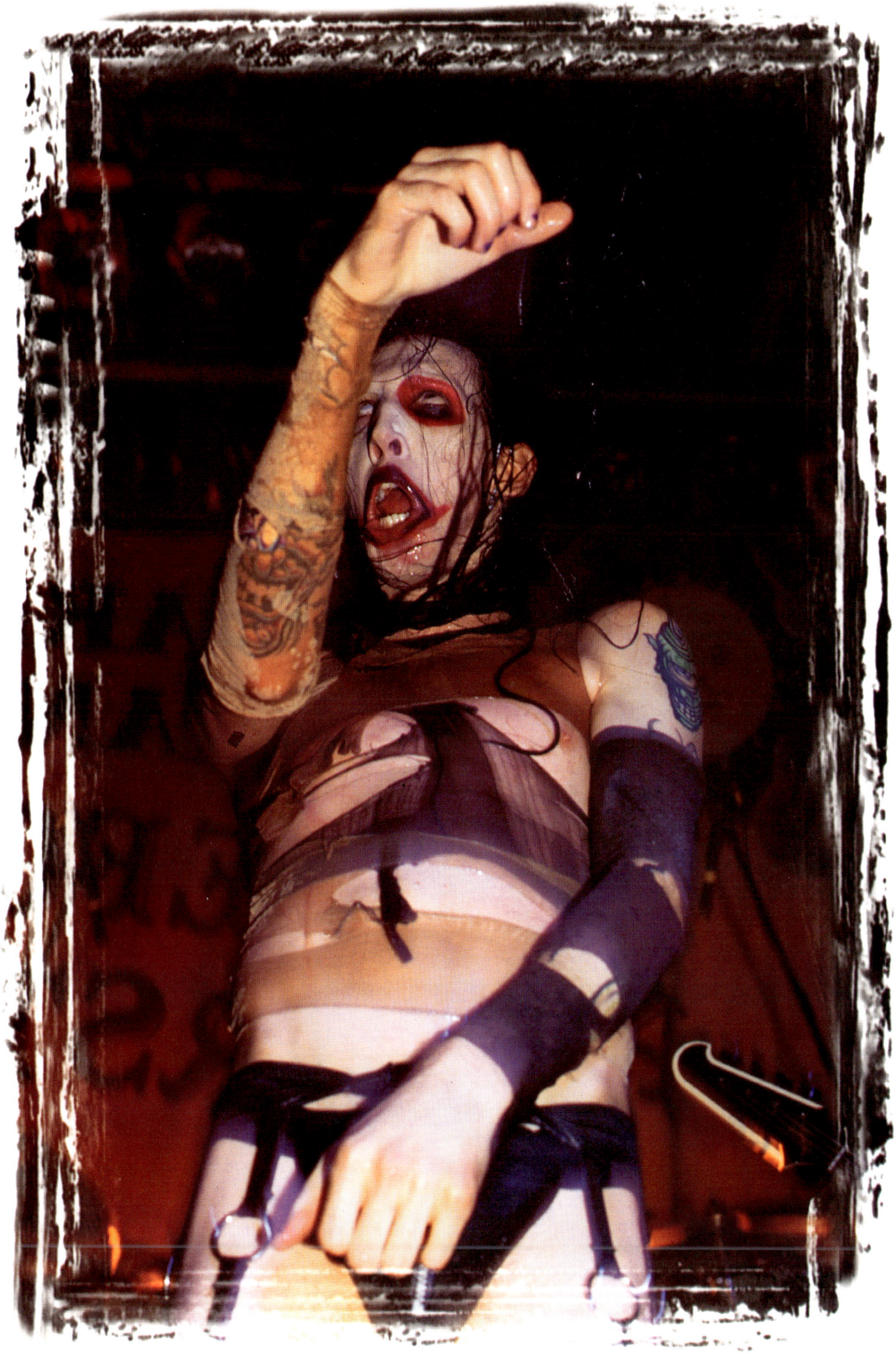

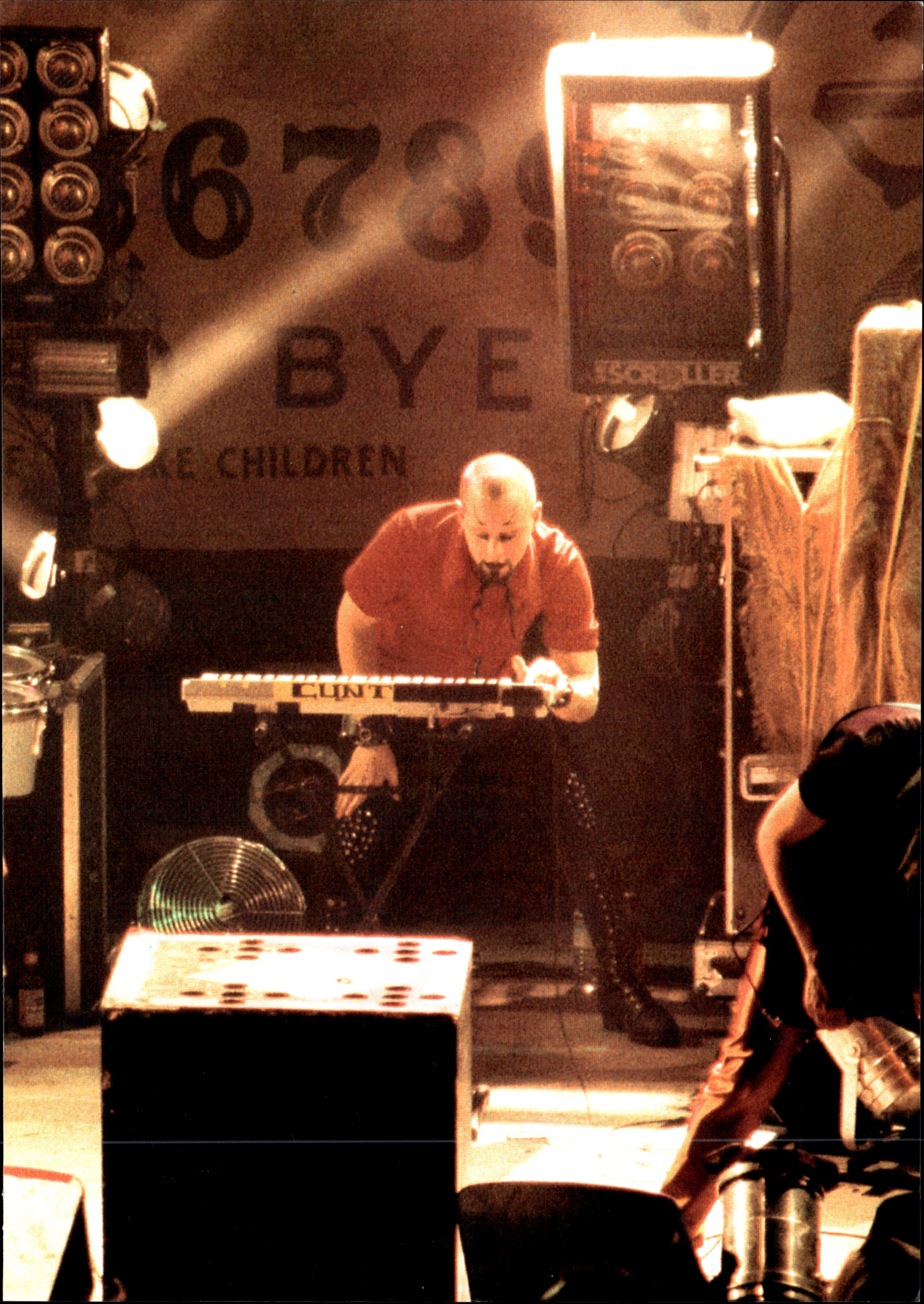
BYE
CHILDREN
CUNT

# PRELUDES and PREMONITIONS

Once upon a time, in a land called Ohio, the future "antichrist superstar" was born and christened Brian Warner. His childhood was, by all accounts, as normal as the next. So when did little Brian begin his metamorphosis into Marilyn Manson? Is it possible to trace his medical accessories fetish to Manson's mother's nursing career or to the numerous times her rather sickly son was hospitalized with pneumonia? Can his tending-toward-obsessive fondness for self-mutilation and disfigurement and his disjointed, crippled stage movements be attributed to the times he and his Vietnam Vet father spent in government tests and meetings regarding the effects of Agent Orange? These events undoubtedly played a part in forming the Marilyn Manson of today. The articulate rock star whose main philosophy is one of individuality also admits to having enjoyed an upbringing he has often cited as being supportive of his unconventional ways.

His early days seem to have been a fair mix of dark and light. Manson's recollections run the gamut of Willie Wonka–influenced happiness to hints of trouble and trauma. He has been oft quoted as remarking that abuse comes in many forms, not all of which are physical. "My father had a very violent temper, and he was never home. So I was kind of a mama's boy," Manson disclosed to *Rolling Stone* in its January 23, 1997, cover story on the band. He went on to confess, "I wish I could go back and change the way I treated my mom because I used to be really rude to her." Furniture salesman Hugh Warner's present-day role seems to be bursting-with-pride father. Warner Senior, who has been known to attend quite a number of Marilyn Manson gigs, announced to *Alternative Press* in its February 6, 1997 issue that, "I knew he was going to be great, whatever he did. He's very dedicated, he does 100 percent. And I'm very proud of him - he's the 'God of Fuck.'" An odd mixture of the comments section of a teacher's pet's report card, the recollections of childhood neighbors of the President, and a token bit of Manson-inspired profanity—but the words of an apparently loving 'rent nonetheless. Manson's father was also quoted in *Rolling Stone*'s June 26, 1997, issue as stating that his son "wants parents to raise their children right, and that's probably what's wrong with our society today. They don't always give children the freedom or respect they deserve."

The lead singer's first encounter with the stage was all but encouraging although oddly appropriate. Playing the part of Jesus in a school play, the little six-year-old future Marilyn Manson sported only a towel as his son-of-God costume ("I wasn't wearing any underwear because I didn't know any better," he explained to *Q* magazine). The towel was duly ripped off the young Manson's skinny frame, and he was suitably traumatized in front of the entire school. Hmm, such an early account of Christianity-tinged sexual humiliation could explain a few things.

Of the good old days in the private Christian school in which his parents enrolled him, Manson recalled to *Q* magazine in July 1997, "I was ostracized there and did my hardest to misbehave and get kicked out. During prayer when everybody had their heads bowed I used to steal money out of the girl's purses. There was one time I put a vibrator in my bible teacher's desk." One doubts whether that childish prank was greeted with a "kids will be kids" shrug—we must assume that the future Reverend Manson wasn't caught red-handed on that occasion. "I used to do a lot of things that, now that I look back on them, were kind of amusing," he reminisced to *Metal Edge* magazine in August 1997. "I would set up myself as a candy dealer, like your modern-day drug dealers, because the kids weren't allowed to have gum in Christian school, and I would peddle it to them at overcharged prices."

When, how, and why the ringleader-to-be began to question the value of authority and convention and to form his own burgeoning view of a different kind of society is impossible to pinpoint. One thing is for certain; Brian Warner would most definitely fulfill the wish he would later howl in song: "I wanna grow up/I wanna be/a big rock and roll star."

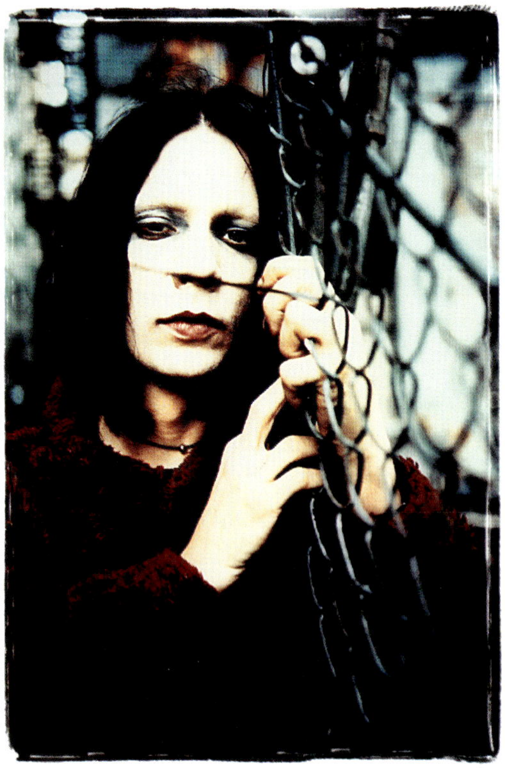

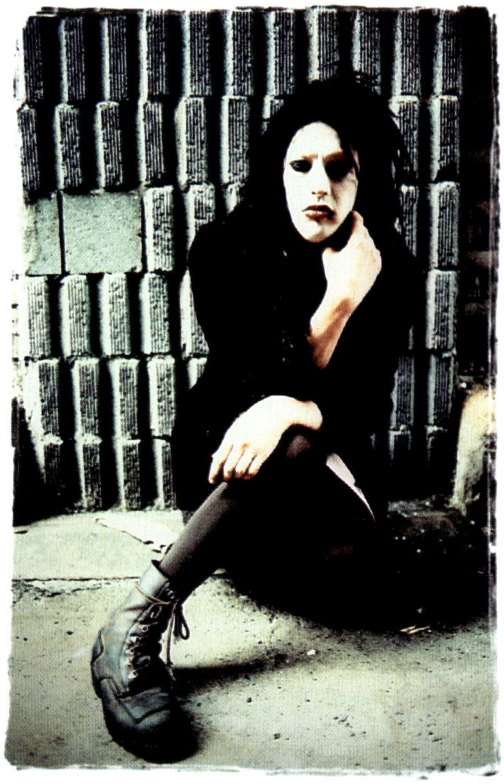

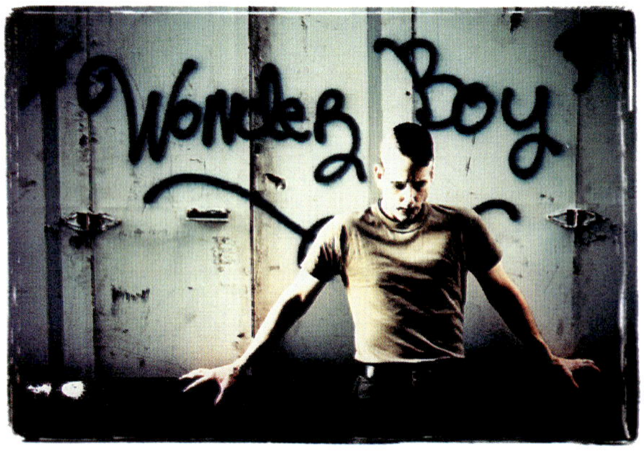
Wonder Boy

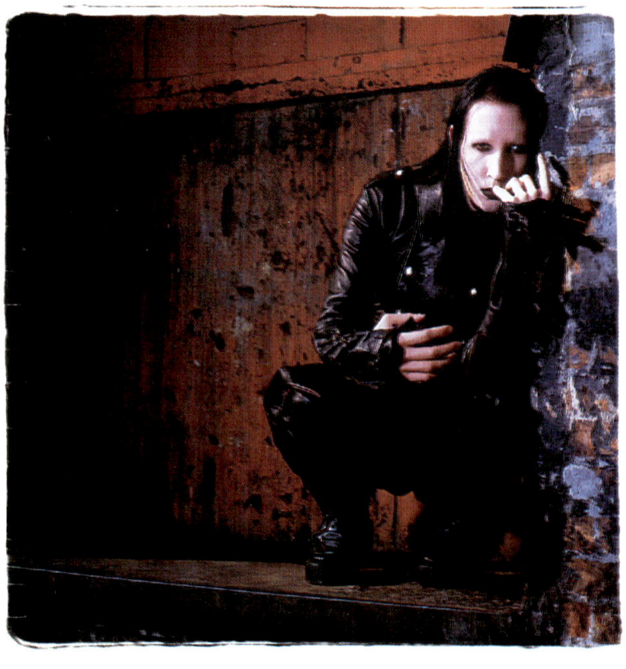

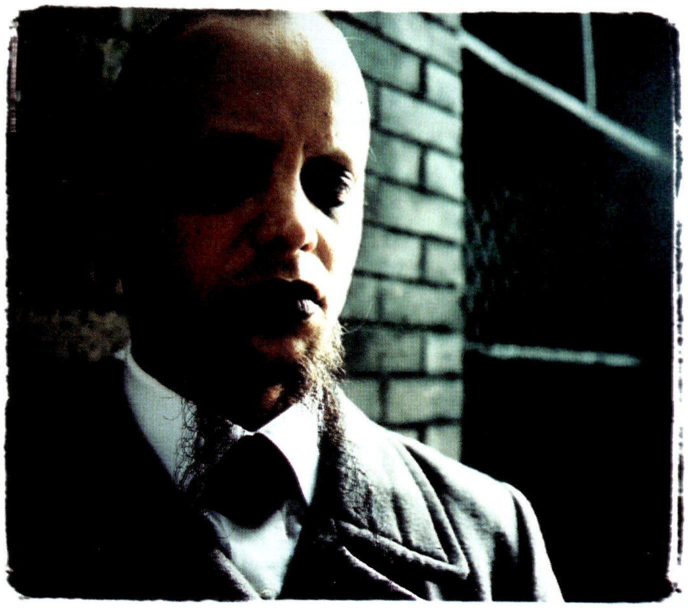

# the CHOCOLATE FACTORY

The first meeting between the creators of a band that would terrorize the right wing of the United States is, alas, undocumented. However, it is known that Manson, sick and tired of his stint as a music journalist, met up with like-minded Daisy Berkowitz, and the two decided to create a mad mixture of music, theater, and mayhem together; hence Marilyn Manson and the Spooky Kids was established in 1989. The name Marilyn Manson "was a pseudonym I had taken on because it kind of defined my style, what I was saying," Manson explained to *Guitar World* in December 1996, adding, "And phonetically, the way it flows, it almost sounds like 'abracadabra.' It has real power to it." One of the musical venture's concepts was the idea behind combining the opposites and celebrating the extremes of life and in doing so pushing it all to the limit. Years later Manson rationalized to *Circus* magazine in its June 17, 1997, issue, "Light and darkness, life and death are simply two inseparable parts of life. . . . Good and evil go hand in hand." And what better way to illustrate this point than by joining two all-American icons, Marilyn Monroe and Charles Manson? Daisy Duke of TV's *The Dukes of Hazzard* and "Son of Sam" murderer David Berkowitz provided the inspiration for Daisy Berkowitz's new title, and the first two Spooky Kids were ready to hit the streets for the trick-or-treat campaign of the century.

The band's earliest incarnation was allegedly the four-man, one-drum machine ensemble that featured Manson and Berkowitz along with bassist Olivia Newton Bundy (Aussie songstress Olivia Newton John and Ted Bundy—put to death in Florida that very year) and Zsa Zsa Speck (the one and only Zsa Zsa Gabor and nurse-murderer Richard Speck). The official line-up took form before the start of 1990 however, with two new, more permanent members who were quite happy to adopt the surname of a murderer and the first name of a female icon, and hence Gidget Gein took over on bass while Madonna Wayne Gacy took his stance behind the keyboards. The Gidget and Madonna monikers surely need no explanation; Ed Gein was a cannibal and John Wayne Gacy the killer of thirty-three young boys.

Marilyn Manson and the Spooky Kids put on quite a show right from the start. Squeeze—a small Fort Lauderdale, Florida, club—was host to many of the band's early gigs, some of which have since become legendary due to word-of-mouth, hype and exaggeration, and even bootlegged videos—filmed by the band's first camcorder-clutching fans—since copied and circulated in trading circles. Jack Kearney, Squeeze's owner (who gets a mention in the "thanks" section of the band's first album), recounted to *Rolling Stone* in its June 26, 1997, issue that at one 1990 gig Manson "had a girl named Terry tied to the cross and semi-naked" and added that, in true telephone-game style, before the night was over the incident had been exaggerated to the point that "[people] were saying she was totally naked and her throat was cut." Of course, the bandmembers—and bandleader—have become more and more outrageous, visually and idealistically, as Marilyn Manson's career has progressed, and such initial Florida gigs in tiny clubs did not, needless to say, present the band in its present-day finery due to the lack of space, high-tech gear, and money to spend on sound, lights, and special effects. However, the core of what makes a Marilyn Manson live show unique was most certainly in evidence at these early shows. Mr. Manson himself, sans tattoos and sporting the eyebrows he was born with, may not have immediately appeared as otherworldly and frightening as he does on stage today, but on closer inspection back then it was not difficult to see the dirty rock star about to emerge. His now-familiar battle with the mic-stand was already in full form, and his manic pounding of it against his own chest and shoulders caused the naked little Barbie-type dolls tied to its wires to perform their own accompanying dance.

The alternately articulate interviewee and animal-like performer we all know and love was plain to see right from the start. The incongruence of the future Reverend's howling, driving vocals with his incredibly calm and mild directions to the stage crew (the likes of "Turn down the mic and the monitors, please," or "Hey mister soundman, can you turn up the drums?" were so persuasively delivered that the desired effect was almost immediate) did not seem to phase his early fans who embraced his schizophrenic leanings as one of his unique charms. Already delivering "inspirational"—if a little unclear—speeches (excerpt from the November 1989 Squeeze gig: "What does a man know about his children, you know?" and "What I hear from you people is you come up to me and you say, 'Save the rainforest, save humanity.'. . . What you gotta do is save yourselves."), Manson was no run-of-the-mill death metal dude.

Nor did his band blend into the background. Daisy took to turning up for gigs in pretty little numbers complete with women's wigs. Madonna, affectionately known as Pogo after his murderer's nickname (Wayne Gacy, when not on a killing spree, moonlighted as a clown for children's parties), set up shop on stage with a "Pogo's Playground" tent.

Manson's present-day predilection for on-stage destruction is nothing new; at one early gig at the aforementioned Squeeze he pulled out (amongst other things better left unmentioned) a chain-saw, sawed through some of the set, and apparently put the fear of God into the young woman housed in a cage at the back of the stage. Other antics at this particular show included Manson making what appeared to be a peanut-butter and banana sandwich and tossing it into the cramped crowd and a seemingly simulated sex act between Manson and the caged girl during the crowd favorite "Cake and Sodomy." Of his violent tendencies while performing, Manson would in August 1997 confess to *Metal Edge* magazine that "it's part of the adrenaline of being on stage, there's a real fearlessness and a sense of numbness and immortality, so often I don't know my own strength and my own limits."

A typical Spooky Kids show back then featured "stage sets" chock-a-block with nasty little toys and devilish decorative touches. Sharing the tiny stage with the band on any given night might be a large shaved doll's head on a stake, a Lite-Brite set spelling out the charming message "Anal Fun," an enormous hat festooned with banners and flowers, an American flag, or a music stand from which Manson might pause momentarily to read aloud from Dr. Seuss's *The Cat in the Hat*. Bloodied and dirty children's clothing was festively hung from a clothesline with care. All of this was but a teensy taste of what was to come.

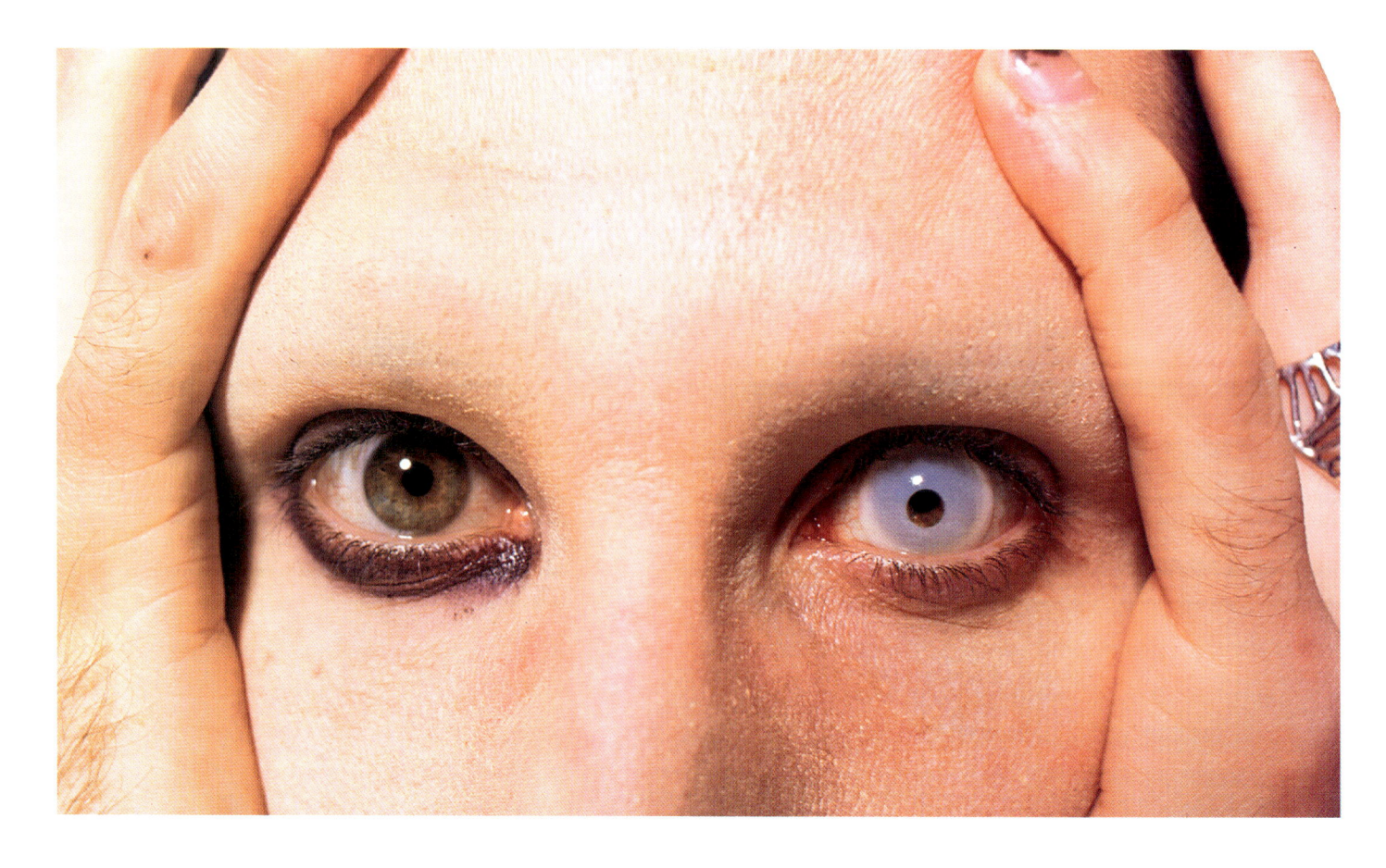

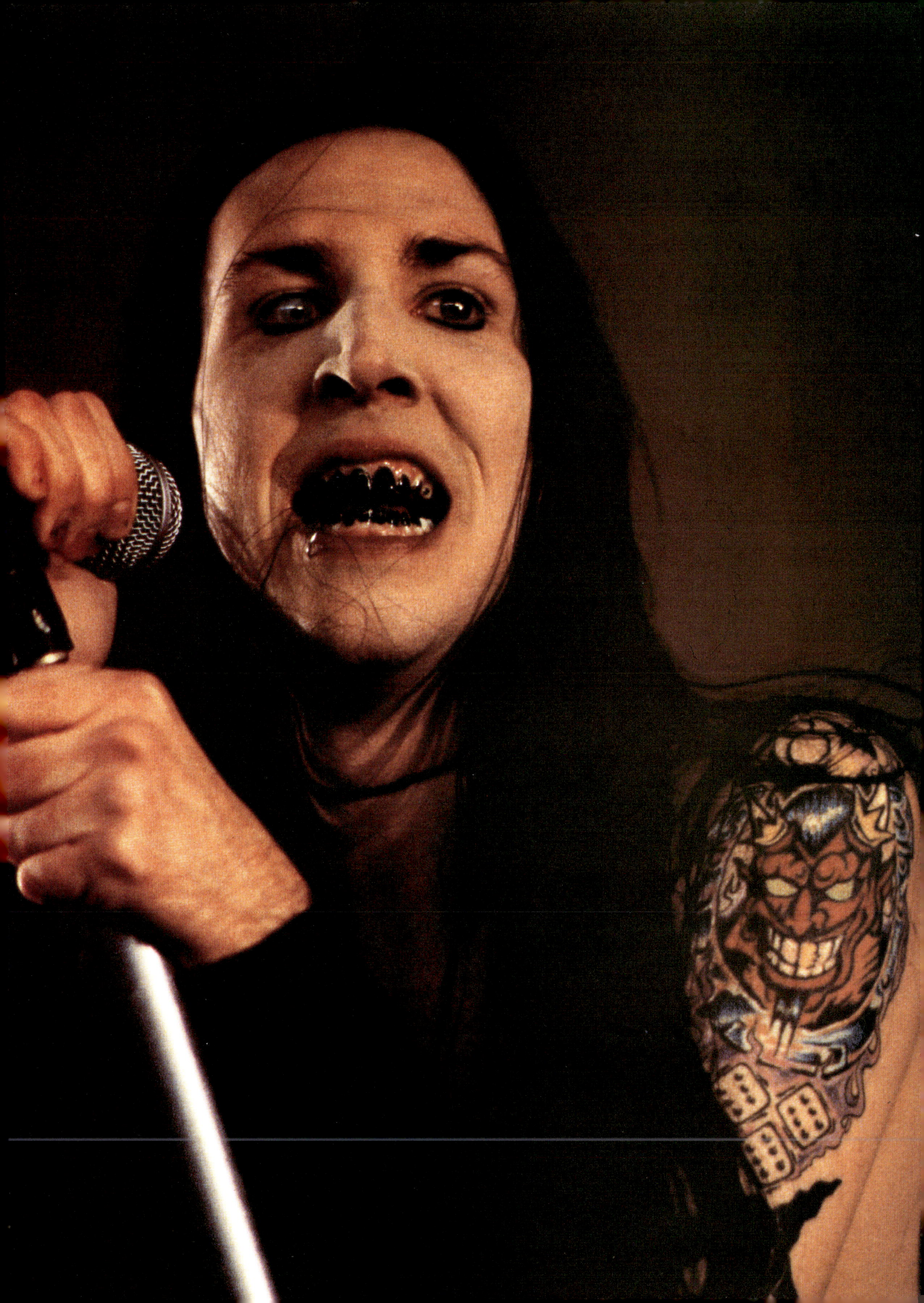

# ABRACADABRA

At the time, however, it seems that a little madcap kick-up-the-ass was just what the doctor ordered for the Florida death-metal scene. In the midst of a revolving roster of misery merchants, another black-haired, tattooed Satanist with a scary voice and a dislike of sunlight was unlikely to cause heads to turn. It was the Marilyn Manson entertainment ethic that stood out from the crowd. And the band didn't stop at creatively conjuring up outrageous stage antics and props. They began building a little empire, a sort of Spooky Kids Experience that took it upon itself to pop up here, there, and everywhere. By performing live on local radio and publishing and distributing their own flyers featuring artwork by Manson himself they further promoted the concept of Marilyn Manson so that the band took on a larger identity. Fans could even take a little spookiness home after the show - the group may not have had a commercial release, but why let that stop them? They produced their own "promotional" cassettes and sold them at gigs. Those very same cassettes, limited in number even then, have now taken on enormous collector's value as well as near-mythical status. Whispers of the existence of the earliest cassettes, entitled *Big Black Bus* (in honor of the original Manson family's mode of transportation), *The Meat Beat Cleaver Set*, *Grist-O-Line*, and *Snuffy's VCR* can be heard at any meeting of self-respecting Manson fans. The band continued this tradition well into 1993 with the more officially documented *After School Special*, *Lunchbox*, *The Family Jams*, and *Refrigerator* tapes. Although there are these days duplicate copies in circulation, the rare originals—design and artwork courtesy of Manson and Berkowitz—are treasured by precious few.

The earliest documented Manson flyer heralded the inauguration of the fifth member of the Spooky Kids and the band's first human drummer. The now-immortalized "Marilyn Manson & the Spooky Kids: The Family Trip to Mortville" brochure announced the arrival of new family member Sarah Lee Lucas, duly credited with "baked goods, percussion." Such a wholesome namesake had yet to be chosen, and the coffee-cake-plying Sarah Lee was paired with the heinous Henry Lee Lucas without further ado. The Mortville flyer featured staple sketch subjects—from the pen of Marilyn Manson himself—lunchboxes, guns, and needles. Perhaps suitably threatening imagery for Sarah Lee, whose days with the band were numbered.

With a live drummer backing the band, the Spooky Kids' own brand of lunatic's special music began to form up quite nicely, thank you. Crowd favorites "Cake and Sodomy" (with its ever-popular "I am the god of fuck" Charles Manson quote), "My Monkey," and even strangely twisted covers of ditties like Black Sabbath's "Iron Man" were hummed on the way home, as it were, and even taught to kids as bedtime lullabies. You may scoff, but the nursery-rhyme cadence of "My Monkey" ("I had a little monkey / I sent him to the country and I fed him on gingerbread / Along came a choo-choo, knocked my monkey coo-coo / And now my monkey's dead") caught the fancy of a fan's son, and six-year-old Robert Pierce not only sang on the track when it was recorded for the band's first album, but also made a guest appearance in the "Lunchbox" video.

The Spooky Kids carried on terrorizing and tantalizing the humid, mosquito-filled swamplands of Southern Florida with their outrageously entertaining freak show. Amidst all of the asylum-style showmanship and maniacal backstage partying, the band was becoming a tighter and better outfit musically, and their notoriety was growing and growing. The Florida metal music scene did not kowtow to middle of the road, run of the mill, sissies-only kudos like the Grammies, and had as the ultimate tribute its own Slammy Awards ceremony. In 1992, Marilyn Manson and company took home two skull-shaped trophies for Band of the Year and Best Hard Alternative Band. Notably, another winner that year was one Jeordie White, who claimed the Best Rhythm Guitarist Slammy for his riffs with black metal band Amboog-A-Lard. As White, now known as Twiggy Ramirez, was to tell *Rolling Stone* in its January 23, 1997, issue, "The day I met him [Manson], I knew we

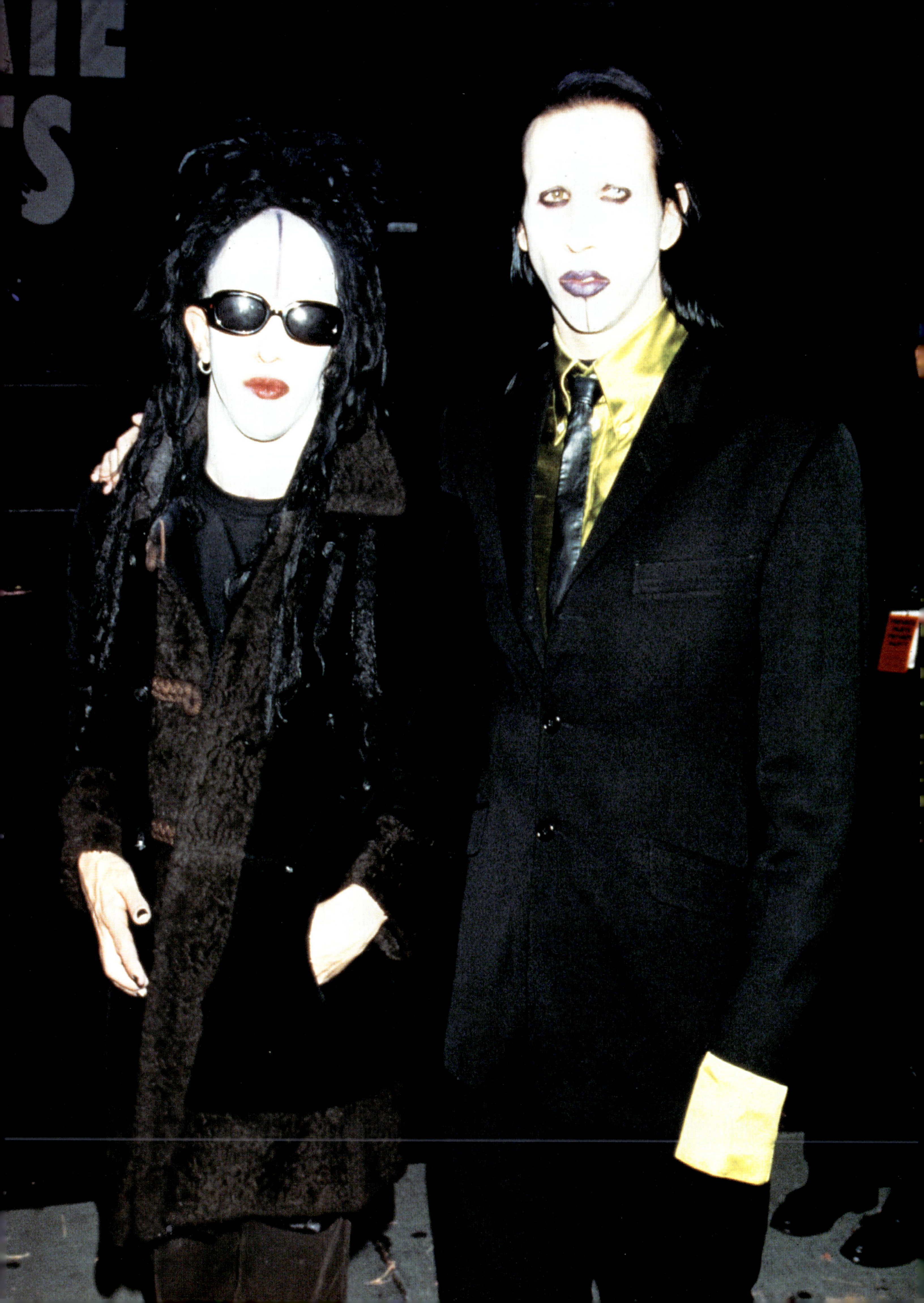

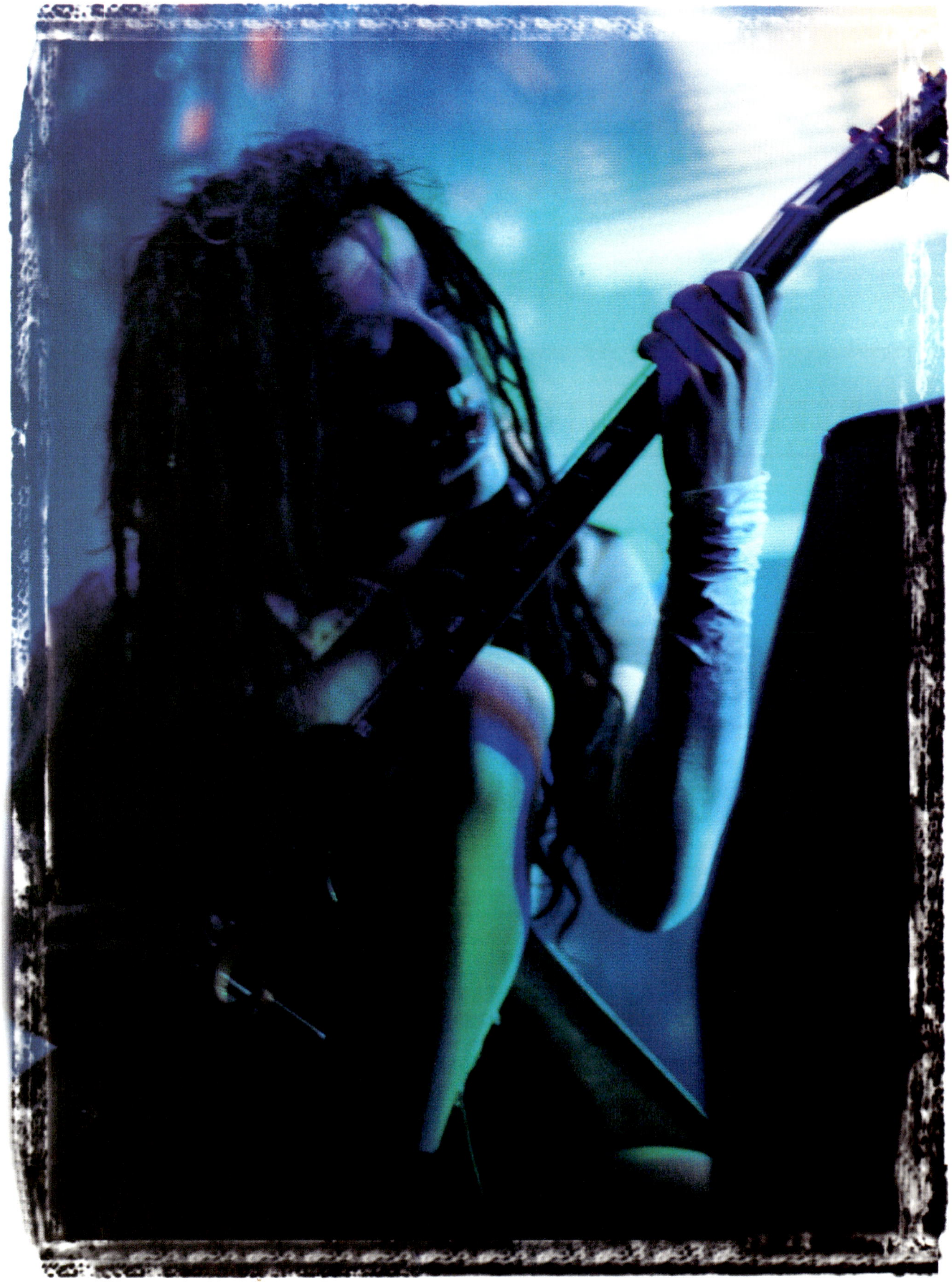

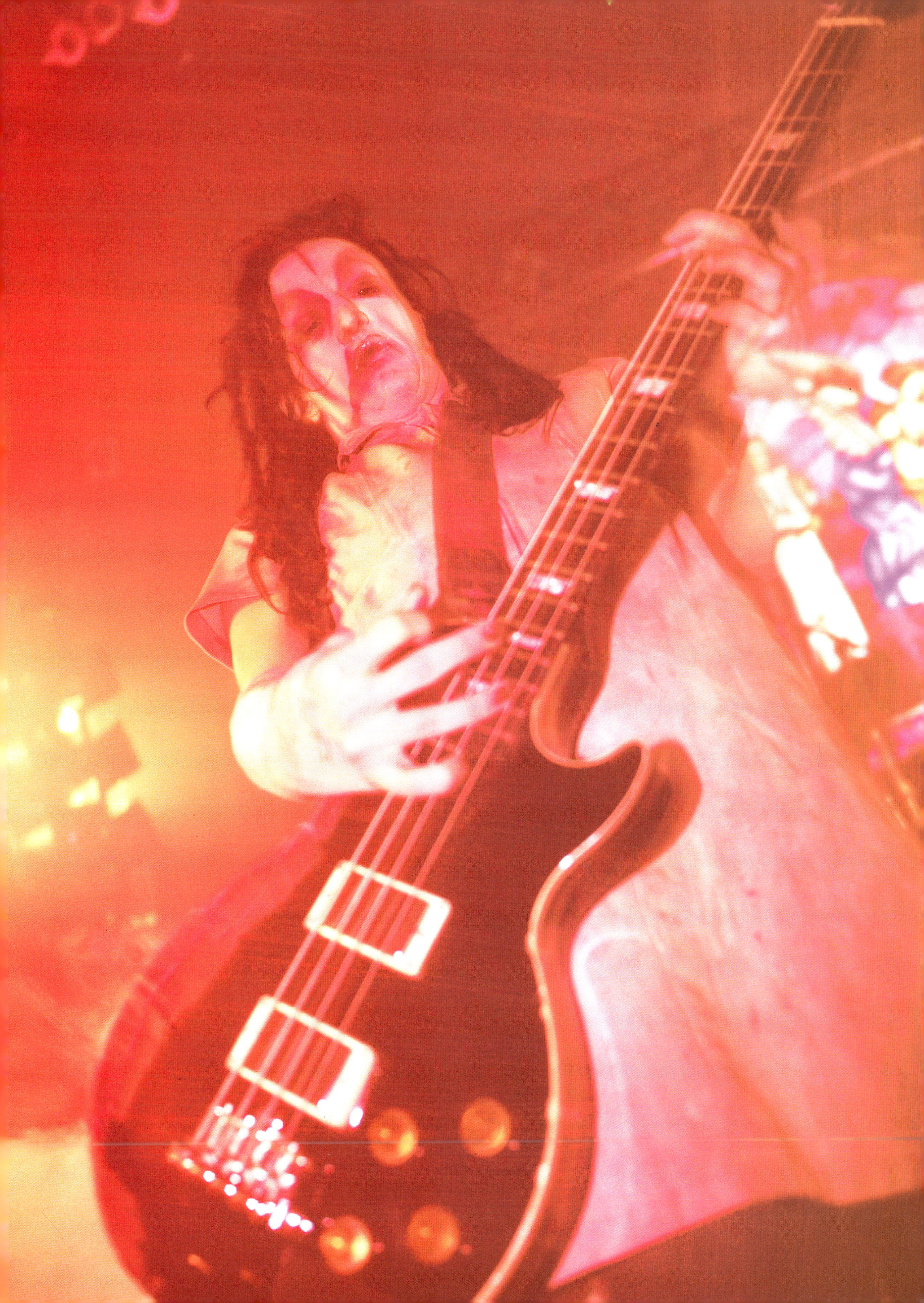

would work together. As the band gained popularity locally, I thought it was my place to either be in the band or destroy it." After Marilyn Manson (the band had shed its Spooky Kids skin for a more stream-lined image, and its lead singer had become simply Mr. Manson) had garnered two more Slammies in 1993—Band of the Year yet again and Song of the Year for "Dope Hat"—Twiggy Ramirez opted, in true "if you can't beat 'em, join 'em" style, to sign on. By December of 1993, he had officially become the bassist for Marilyn Manson, replacing Gidget whose drug addiction is often blamed for his departure from the band. Of his name, Twiggy would later tell *Guitar World* in December 1996, "I like Richard Ramirez because he was into heavy metal music. And I chose Twiggy because she was androgynous. She liked to dress up like a little boy."

Manson's first meeting with his true right-hand man allegedly took place in that all-American institution, the shopping mall. Mr. Manson—perhaps on a reconnaissance mission of sorts—bumped into the future Twiggy, and the pair began mischief-making post haste. The gruesome twosome's maiden deviant joint venture was to torment an unsuspecting young female shopkeeper with death-threats and prank calls from a payphone a few feet away from their prey. Their efforts soon expanded beyond such fairly run-of-the-mill adolescent antics, and they jump-started two musical projects together. Twiggy (masquerading as a woman) was the lead singer in Mrs. Scabtree, with Manson on drums. More interesting, however, is their other undertaking, the bogus Christian metal group Satan on Fire, whose inspired single was entitled "Mosh for Jesus."

# INAUGURATION

It was in May of 1993 that Trent Reznor extended the party invitation of a lifetime to Mr. Manson and his troupe. A collegiate journalism major, Manson allegedly interviewed his future mentor Reznor after a Nine Inch Nails gig in Florida, and as his own music became increasingly influential and critically acclaimed, Reznor had not failed to keep his ears pricked for other bands' sounds. Reznor's invitation to Manson that he and his band be the premiere act on his new Nothing label was fittingly extended at none other than the "Manson Mansion," the site of the horrific murder of Sharon Tate committed by the hands of the original Manson Family in 1969. Reznor had unwittingly (and if you believe that . . .) rented the house to use as his studio. Nothing Records would soon be the home of quite a few other bands, notably Coil, Meat Beat Manifesto, Prick, Pig, and the trailblazing UK group Pop Will Eat Itself, but Marilyn Manson was the very first family member, and just to make the occasion that much sweeter, Reznor threw in the opening spot on the upcoming Nine Inch Nails 1994 "Self Destruct" tour.

And so it was that the former Spooky Kids got down to business. Early publicity shots of the band show a much more colorful, much less frightening version of the fearful five. Manson can be found in red vinyl peacoat and candystripe tights clutching a lunchbox and looking for all the world like an apprehensive little kid, hair freshly brushed and parted by mom, in the driveway having his picture snapped before his first day of school. Madonna in rapper snow hat featuring the logo TWAT, Daisy looking frighteningly like Elvis Costello with long hair, and Twiggy in faux leopard-skin cap and coat over a baseball uniform complete the picture of a band packed and ready for a trip.

Capturing the showmanship and abandon of the Marilyn Manson sound on tape was not an easy task. The group set up shop at Criteria Studios in Miami to work on their first official album release, scheduled to hit the stores in July 1994. All did not, as they say, come up roses, however, and Manson was frustrated to hear the signature madman's-day-out music he'd spent years cultivating all but disappear after production and mixing were completed. The disappointing results were duly handed over to Reznor in California who took over as Executive Producer and whipped the sessions into shape. The outcome was the thirteen track collection of Manson gems entitled *Portrait of an American Family*.

The album cover, sporting a well-deserved "Parental Advisory" logo, should certainly have prepared first-time listeners for something just a little different, just a bit deranged, outrageous, and twisted. The portrait is a scene handmade by Mr. Manson featuring a doll family of four seated in their own hideously American family room. The father doll, complete with undershirt, beer, and cigarette, sports a belt buckle of a fist wrapped around a gun with the delightful logo, "Nobody Ever Raped a .38" The sleeve artwork, made up of scary Manson sketches and band photos, features a disturbed-looking young boy with a red-lipstick-smeared face clutching a needle in front of the "Manson TV"—this is Twiggy's little brother. Twiggy is listed as a band member, acknowledged for "Base Tendencies," although Gidget Gein is credited for "all bass played on this recording."

The CD itself, stamped with the "You cannot sedate all the things you hate" slogan, is a full-on, fun and fury-fueled ride on the Marilyn Manson boat to hell. As Manson knows all too well, no self-respecting kiddie watched Willie Wonka's psychedelic boat ride sequence in *Charlie and the Chocolate Factory* without feeling a little freaked out, and he brings the listener back to childhood fear with the opening track, "Prelude (The Family Trip)." It is a terrifying take on the film's scene, with Manson whispering "There's no earthly way of knowing/Which direction we are going/Not a speck of light is showing/So the danger must be growing." Suitably set up, the onslaught of samples, soundbites, warped and wonderful sounds, and songs with titles like "Organ Grinder," "Misery Machine," "Snake Eyes and Sissies," and "Wrapped in Plastic" begins.

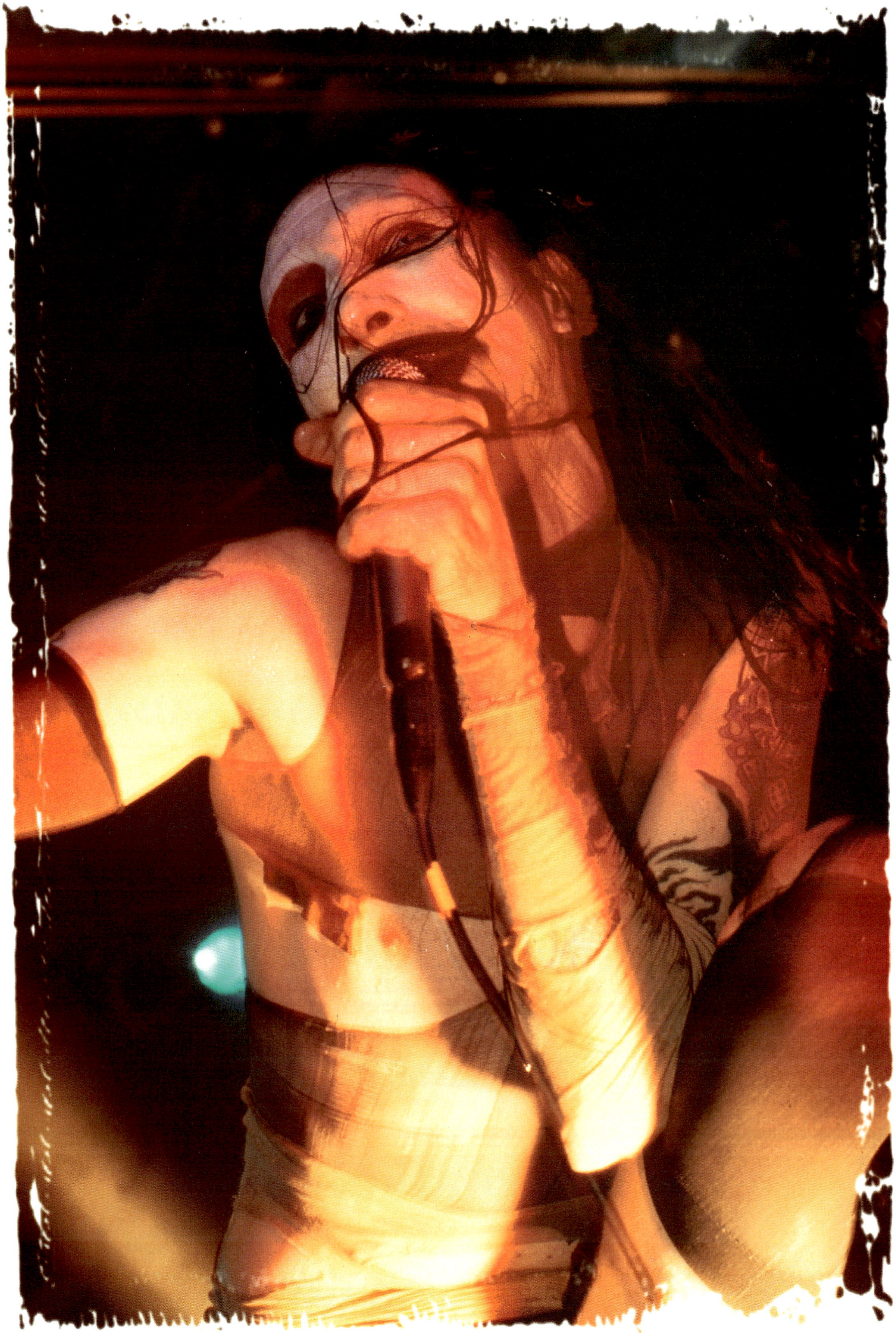

Manson's voice growls, screams, and hisses its way through lyrics inspired by magic tricks, society's ills, Charles Manson, Willie Wonka, sex, drugs, and rock 'n' roll. The album closes with a hidden track in the form of an answering machine message recorded on the Marilyn Manson Family Intervention Hotline (407-997-9437—now sadly defunct). The voice of an infuriated woman demanding that her son be removed from the band's mailing list is the final word; she snarls, "I have already contacted the post office for your pornographic material that is being received in the mail. My next stop is my attorney." The threatening message rounds off the album with a heartfelt "Thank you and good-bye!"

The chosen single, a little dittie called "Get Your Gunn" which has as its radio-friendly subject matter the abortion issue, was written about gynecologist Dr. David Gunn who was murdered by pro-life protestors. The song, with its relentless chorus "I hate therefore I am/Goddamn your righteous hand," also appears on the soundtrack to the film *S.F.W. (So Fucking What?)*. References to just how screwed up American society has become abound on the album. The song "Lunchbox," a truly classic Manson piece, decries the horrible absurdity of the law passed eradicating metal lunchboxes as they were bound to be used as weapons—this in a country where metal detectors are in place at schools to stop kids from bringing the family pistol in for "show and tell." Manson takes on yet another persona as he sings, "The big bully try to stick his finger in my chest/try to tell me, tell me he's the best/but I don't really give a good goddamn 'cause/I got my lunchbox and I'm armed real well." The Manson recipe of nursery rhymes and heavy metal, tomfoolery and tirades, and a pinch of pins and needles is cooked up nice and hot here in the band's debut, and served American-style.

A Fallout Films promotional video to the tune of the track "Dope Hat" was produced. Directed by Tom Stern, the psychotic and psychedelic video is a visual adaptation of Willie Wonka's boat ride, with the Manson troupe, drum set and all, playing the song as they wind their way along the water. On board is a cane-wielding top-hatted Mr. Manson, a frightened boy and girl tied to their seats, and what looks to be the original Oompa-Loompas from the famed film alternately rowing the boat, singing along, dancing, and pouring maple syrup onto women's bodies. After the boat has left candyland and entered the tunnel, nightmarish apparitions float by: miscellaneous pieces of fruit cut open to reveal live mice, maggots, or wriggling fish; Manson disemboweling a medical student's doll; a headless plucked chicken dancing about; a human body writhing on a flaming barbecue; and a doll whose eyes are pulled out by a pair of pliers. One particularly nasty aside is of Marilyn Manson licking drawings of people along to the subtitles, "The girls taste like girls. The boys taste like boys." Even the usually more reserved Daisy participates in a bit of scarifying facial contortions and generally gets into the spirit of things in this wild and wigged-out video which unfortunately will never see the light of VH-1 but which nevertheless is quite a piece of work.

True to form, Mr. Manson could not resist accompanying the professional, big-time manifestations of Marilyn Manson with a little homespun promotion, and hence the publication of the biggest, baddest Manson flyer yet—"The Marilyn Manson Family Reality Transmission M1 (Fall 1994)." A full-scale Declaration of Independence, Manson-style, this clever and amusing ouevre manages to pronounce the band's philosophy, provide a few good laughs, and put down the "bible-belt-wearing-pro-life-red-neck-record-burning-fundamental-fag-bashing hypocrites." Not bad for starters. It contains a proliferance of believe in yourself doctrines, claiming that "Marilyn Manson rejects conventional morality and society's self-serving standards. When WE become the majority, we will decide who 'doesn't belong.'" Charmingly illustrated with Manson sketches of syringes, razor blades, shotguns, lunchboxes, and even a "Satanic Army" van, this is nothing if not a good read. Added features are an "Advised Reading and Listening" section along with a "Things to Keep You Busy" contest. And as the world was to learn, Manson's no fool; disclaimers abound, to the tune of "Be creative. Disregard the law. Don't tell anyone we told you to" and "You must pay in responsibility. If you listen to Marilyn Manson and m!urder your family you will go to jail. That's reality. If you decide to commit suicide for a song—So Long Sucker! That kind of thinking has no place in our movement."

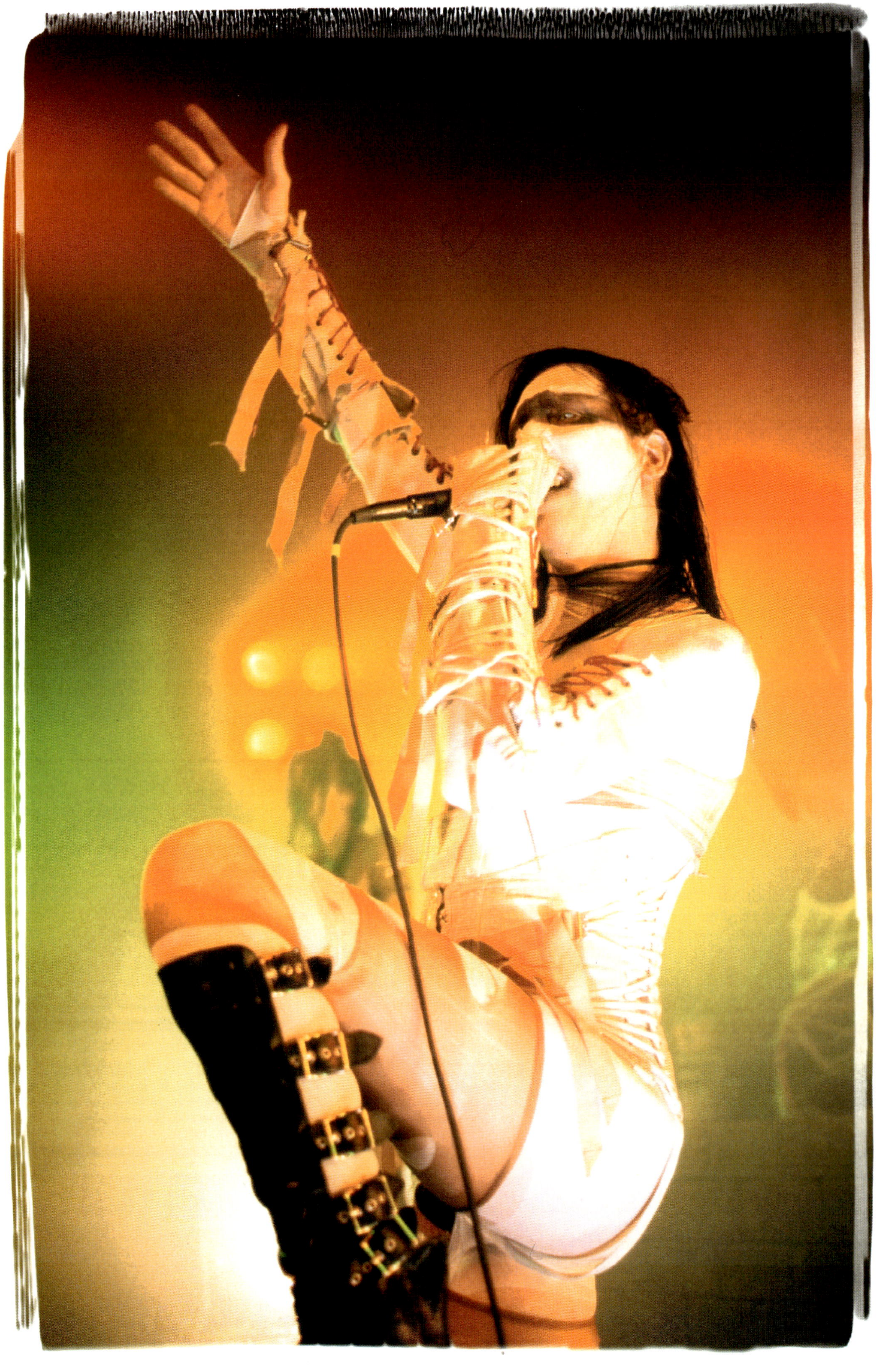

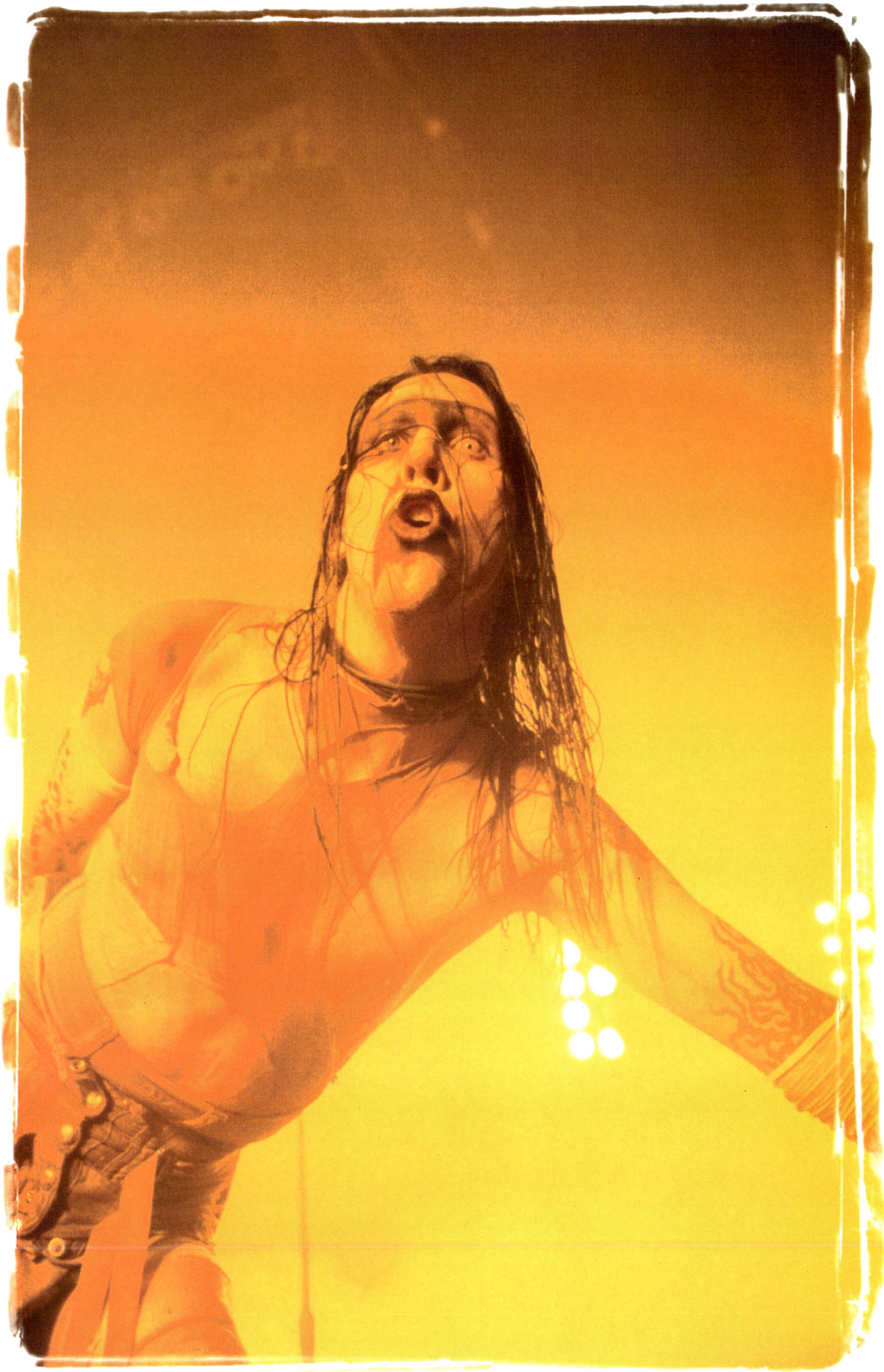

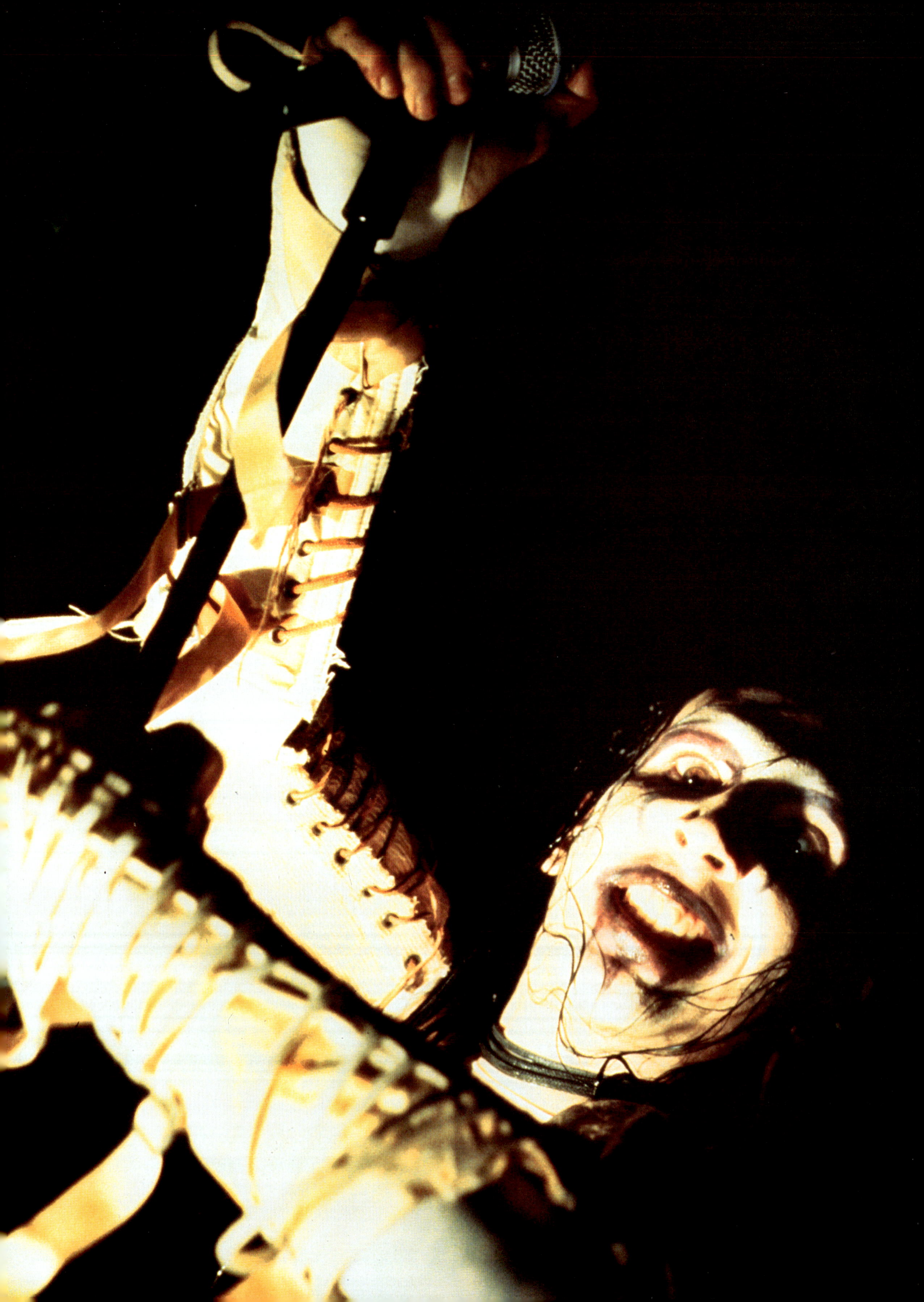

# all HALLOW'S EVE

With an album under their collective belt, Marilyn Manson was primed and positioned to conquer the country on the coattails of none other than King of Nothing, Trent Reznor. The Nine Inch Nails "Self Destruct" tour kicked off in August 1994. Courtney Love's band Hole and the Jim Rose Circus Sideshow were also along for the ride. But what's a good nationwide tour without a spot of devil-worship and a run-in with a major religious group? Rated highly amongst the tour's highlights most certainly was the banning of Marilyn Manson from ever performing in Salt Lake City, Utah, again. As it would turn out, the Mormons didn't take kindly to Manson ripping their Bible apart on stage and flinging the holy pages upon the mosh-pit. Especially as the "Mormon Mafia" had seen him coming and had only booked innocent little Nine Inch Nails' October 18 Delta Center gig on condition that they not bring their evil friends along as support. You see, the lead singer had just been officially named a Priest of the Church of Satan by none other than head honcho Anton LaVey, with whom Manson had a summit meeting on the California leg of the tour. Mr. Manson was thereafter known as Reverend Manson, and the Mormons just weren't having it. Allegedly forfeiting the $10,000 offered to the band not to turn up, the newly ordained Reverend couldn't resist making a surprise appearance. The tour grand-finaleed its way through two nights at New York City's Madison Square Garden in mid December without a further (reported) hitch.

The Mansons decided to go Home for the Holidays, and in their ever-festive spirit celebrated the Yuletide and the New Year with four Florida gigs. And how better to add that special something to Christmastime than by a bit of joyous public exposure and an overnight stay in the slammer? The December 27 Jacksonville Club 5 concert saw the Reverend Manson arrested for "violation of the Adult Entertainment Code" by a gaggle of local cops who just happened to be in the audience. He was hustled off to the closest jail cell and not released until the next morning.

Not a month went by before another disturbance took place. Yes, it was the famed "Chicken Incident" of January 13 in Dallas, Texas, on the second night of Marilyn Manson's headlining tour with Monster Voodoo Machine as support. A chicken, requested innocently enough by the band as a joke and duly provided by the concert promoter, was let loose on stage. United Poultry Concerns, a group who despite their low profile obviously had their fingers on the pulse, immediately heard of the incident and hysterically put forth that "the audience dismembered the live chicken in a bacchanalian orgy of violence."

Well, enough on-stage upsets—how about a nationally televised Marilyn Manson transmission. To wet their chops, in February Manson, Twiggy, and Madonna Wayne Gacy were part of a discussion panel about moshing on the Phil Donahue Show, but it was the guest appearance of the Marilyn Manson crew on the *Jon Stewart Show* on June 22, 1995, the day before the talk show was canceled, that should certainly go down in TV history. The squeaky-clean talk show host announced happily to the camera, "We're ready for some music" before the set's music stage was taken over by the most colorful freak show ever to grace network television before being duly set alight. Yes, you heard right . . . Manson, never one to be caught out without a shot of lighter fluid on hand, actually set fire to the stage while belting out the "I wanna grow up/I wanna be/a big rock and roll star" chorus of "Lunchbox." The fire itself was not nearly as shocking as the onslaught of the five band members, made up and dressed up to the nines for their television appearance. The cameraman, more than likely thrilled at the departure from run-of-the-mill talk show material, followed the outrageous-as-ever Marilyn as he swooped and lunged all over the small stage. Done up in black vinyl trousers, elbow length gloves with red feather-boa trim, and only one eyebrow of sorts to speak of, Mr. Manson presented quite a contrast to the Oriental carpeted set. The unrelenting song was brought to an end by Manson attempting to destroy a mic stand and sundry equipment and the drummer collapsing on the floor behind his drum set. Fairly dramatic, but the true topper took place when Jon Stewart, in true Letterman style, came on stage to say, "There you go folks, Mar—" when he was cut off by the spidery form of Mr. Manson jumping on his back, wrapping himself around his host, attempting to pull his shirt off and covering his mouth with his begloved hands. Stewart, a good sport to be sure, took it all in stride and stamped out the fire (still burning on the floor) with his feet, while Reverend Manson enjoyed a piggyback ride. Amazingly, Stewart welcomed the pyromaniac rock star back to perform "Dope Hat" after telling the audience that before the show a roadie for the band had requested a live chicken "'cause we wanna put it in our bass drum." Warning bells may have been heard going off in a lesser talk show host's head, but hey, the show only had one more night to go.

That was not the only flame-related happening that year; earlier on during their tour the band set fire to Sarah Lee Lucas. Well, they actually lit up his drum kit, but as he was still performing at the time, the fire spread as fires are wont to do, and poor old Sarah Lee bolted from the stage still smoldering, never to return. As Twiggy would later recount to *Circus* magazine, "He sort of wasn't into it, so we never really saw him after that. I know he's alive, we didn't kill him." Manson told *Metal Edge* magazine in August 1997 that despite "the years that I had babied him during his drug addiction, and the many times that I saved his life, I only get hostility and problems from him, and so I wish him nothing but the worst." Not quite an amicable parting, but at least no one was seriously injured.

Sarah Lee's replacement, Ginger Fish (child cannibal Albert Fish and Ginger Rogers), quickly joined up. Ginger had has own rather dubious roots in the entertainment industry; his father was "a crooner who hung out with Frank Sinatra and Paul Anka" according to *Drum!* magazine and his mother a former tap dancer. He himself allegedly had a brief gig drumming in the orchestra pit for, prophetically enough, a production of *Jesus Christ Superstar*. The new drummer, however, was to endure his share of punishment as seemed to be the Marilyn Manson tradition. Fast-forward to the September 7, 1996, "nothing" night at New York City's Irving Plaza when the drummer was sent home by ambulance. Mr. Manson, as is his habit, began whipping his mic stand around wildly and lost control of it; it struck Ginger who stopped drumming for a moment or two. He began playing again only to be struck again by Twiggy's bass. The entire band reportedly left the stage—and Ginger—who crawled out from behind his drum kit before collapsing in a pool of blood before a stunned and silenced audience. Rather than the band bounding back on stage for a triumphant encore, roadies and paramedics emerged from backstage to rouse, drag away, and bandage the injured drummer. An awful way to wind up a gig, but not enough to drive Ginger to safer shores. All in day's work, apparently.

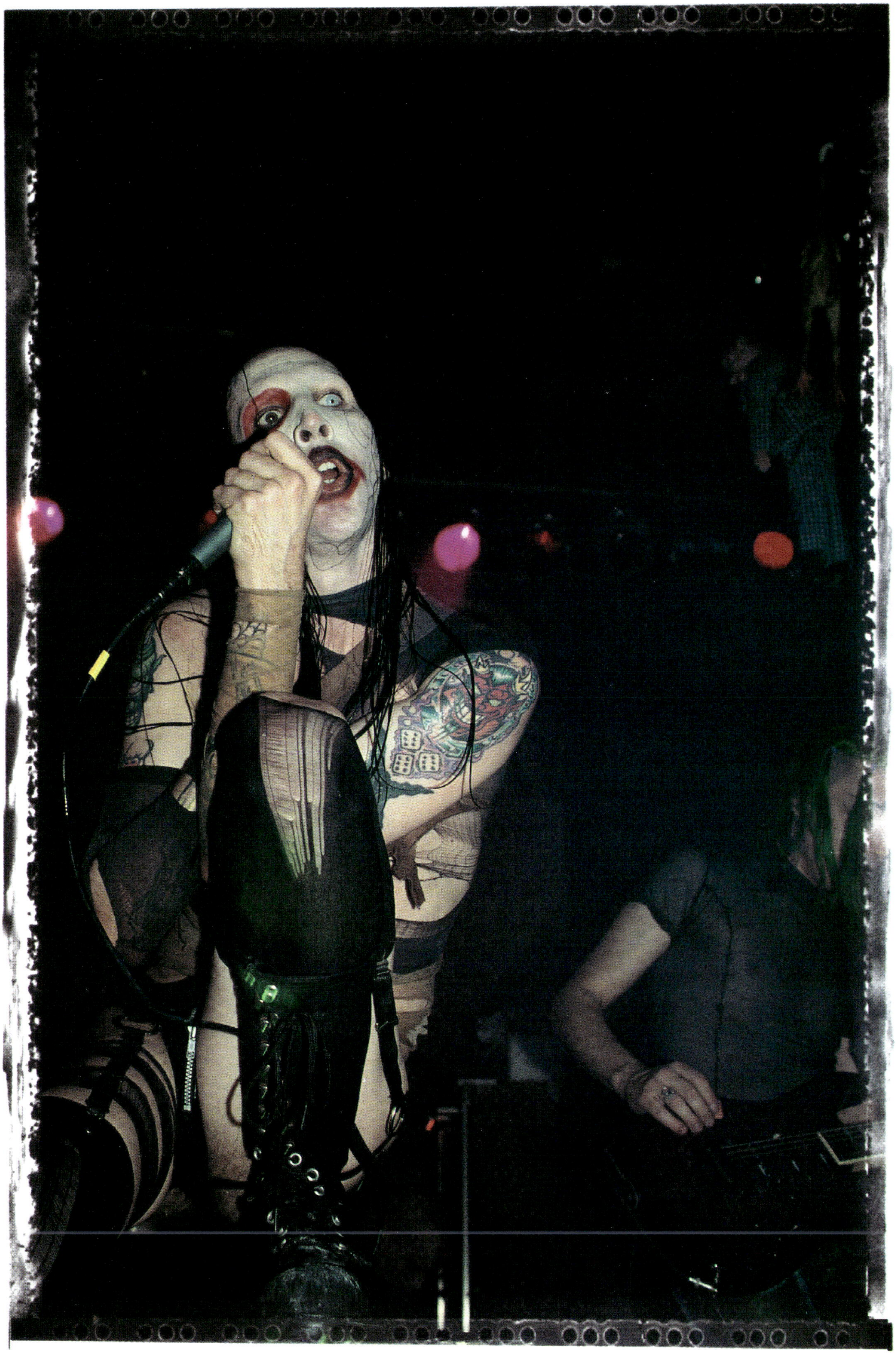

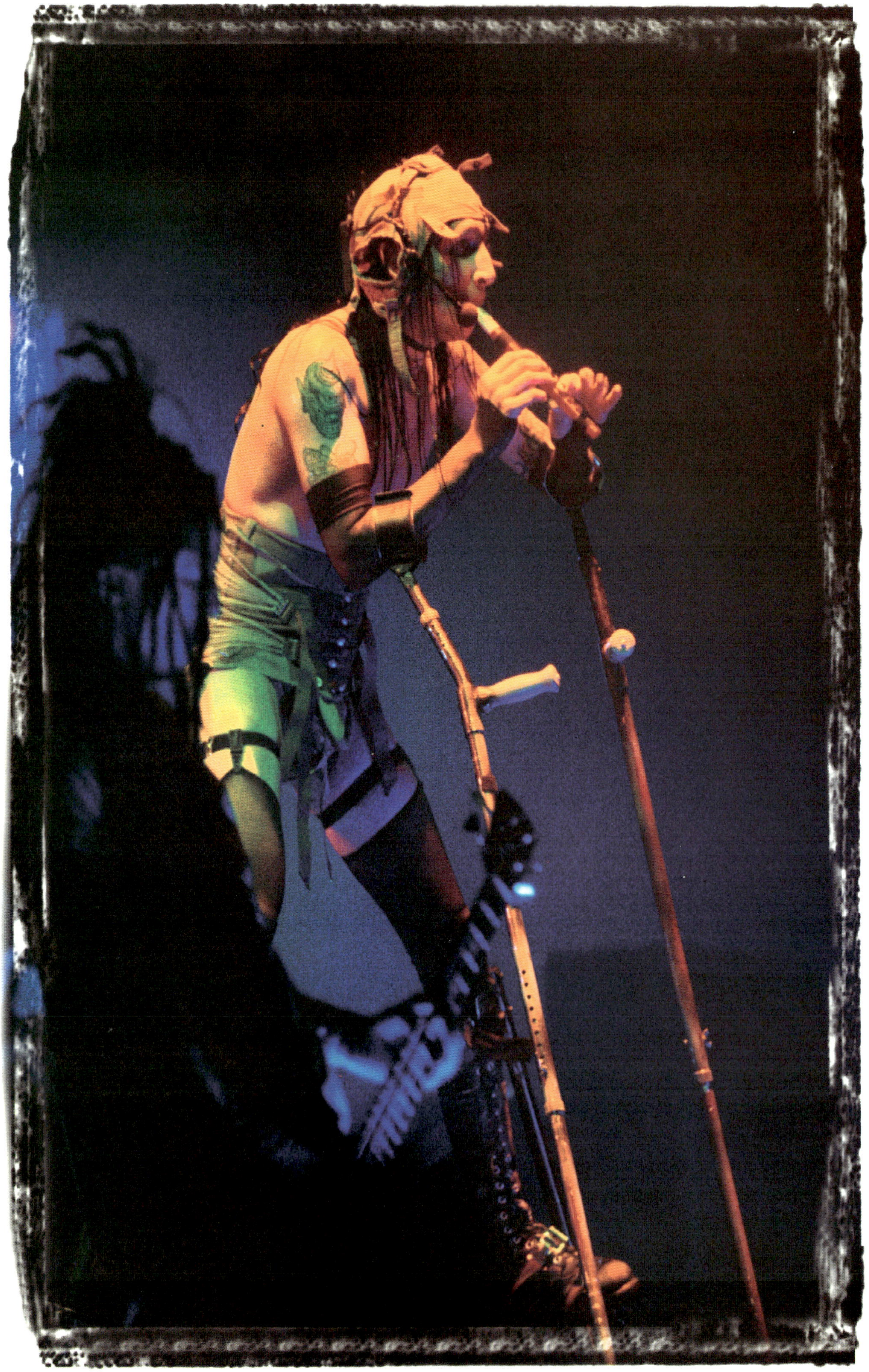

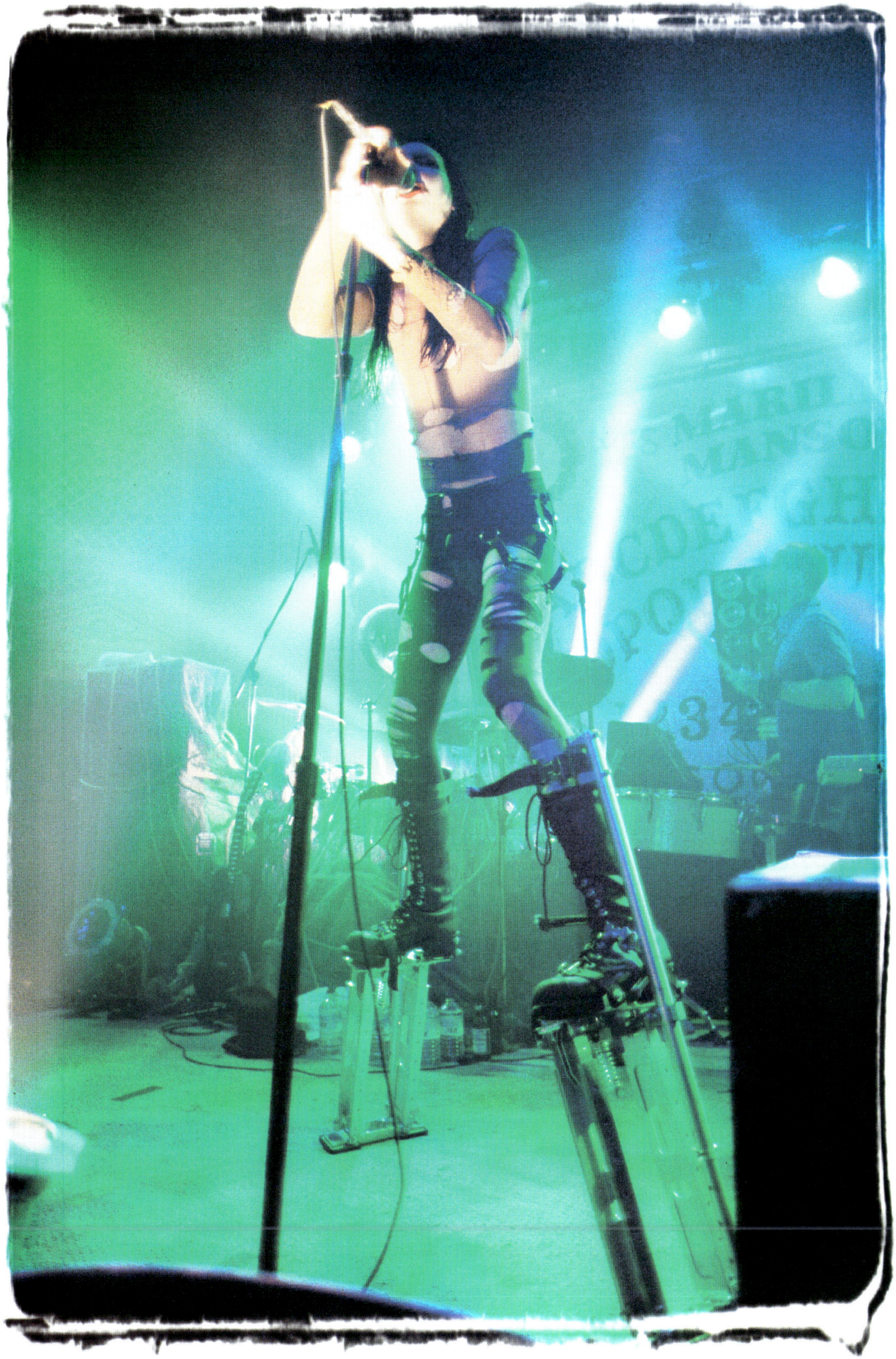

# the CHILD SNATCHERS

Ginger Fish's initiation took place during Marilyn Manson's Spring tour as opening act for Danzig. Once he was suitably broken in, the band pulled off the road to record what turned out to be their first real ice-breaker into the mainstream music scene, the *Smells Like Children* EP. Named for the words of the Child Snatcher from the kiddies' film Chitty Chitty Bang Bang, the EP was intended to simply be the "Dope Hat" single, but once the band started conjuring up remixes of songs from *Portrait*, cover versions, live recordings, and a weird assortment of samples and noises, they found themselves unable to part with any of it. And wisely so. Aside from inspired originals like "S****y Chicken Gang Bang" and "Sympathy for the Parents," the EP featured a number of covers—Patti Smith's "Rock 'n' Roll Nigger" and Screamin' Jay Hawkins's "I Put a Spell on You"—but it was Marilyn Manson's version of the Eurythmics' "Sweet Dreams (Are Made of This)" that started all the trouble.

As Manson would tell *Alternative Press* in its February 6, 1997, issue, "Sweet Dreams" was "just a clever piece of cheese on a rat trap! A lot of innocuous mall shoppers bought 'Sweet Dreams' and were then introduced to this whole new world of Marilyn Manson that they didn't expect. And ultimately that's the most devious thing you could ever pull off." In the age of the MTV Nation, it was the Dean Karr–directed video for the song that brought Marilyn Manson in front of the eyes and ears of a huge audience of music fans who would otherwise not have given the band the time of day. The Manson we have come to know, love, and, in many cases, fear was suddenly on television screens across America in full costume. The image of Manson's lacerated stomach as he wandered half-dressed in a dirty tutu through empty back-streets with a crippled gait was difficult to banish from memory. Howling and whispering the Eurythmics' song through the veil of a full-length wedding dress, riding a wild pig, pounding across the floor on a pair of three-foot stilts, Marilyn Manson had crashed the party. And he wasn't going home until all the beer had been drunk and the place was a wreck.

Now was the time to pull out a few more stops. With *Smells Like Children* hung by the chimney with care, Marilyn Manson began making housecalls, visiting the hometowns of those "innocuous mall shoppers" in the hopes of further reeling them in. The first stop-off on Mission Manson was poor unsuspecting Tulsa, Oklahoma, on September 12, 1995, and the technicolor whirling dervish of a show swept across the country through Texas, New Mexico, California, Colorado, and over to the East Coast and Canada. With bands like Clutch, Hanzel and Gretyl, Halcion, and Johnny SkilSaw in tow, the Spooky Kids brought a show unlike any other to clubs in nearly all major—and quite a few minor—cities. Marilyn Manson brought in the New Year yet again, this time at New York City's The Academy with Lunachicks.

Although Manson had yet to garner any truly massive attention from the media—something not far away on the horizon—word of mouth was doing the trick. Hardcore fans and newcomers alike were deviously delighted with the matchless, shameless show that pushed itself to the extreme. Picture a wide red-lit stage fronting a crowd near-silent in anticipation. The figure of Marilyn Manson, wearing a long black cloak and a tall witch's hat is suddenly spotlit, and the eery figure's white face barely moves as he recites, in an increasingly urgent whisper, the "boat ride" segment from his beloved *Chocolate Factory*. His rasping of "the danger must be growing" reaches a peak and the band erupts into twisted, angry song.

Next up is the glam-rockesque "Dope Hat." The drum-beat-driven haunted-house opening strains are the perfect soundtrack to the silhouette of a top-hatted Manson creeping on-stage wielding a cane. Suspenders long-since shrugged off his naked coat-hanger shoulders to hang from his waist, the spider-like figure appears even more insectlike due to the bulky knee-braces on his painfully thin legs. As he jerks about the stage like a marionette controlled by a puppeteer on acid, his epileptic movements echo the song with amazing precision. Other sig-

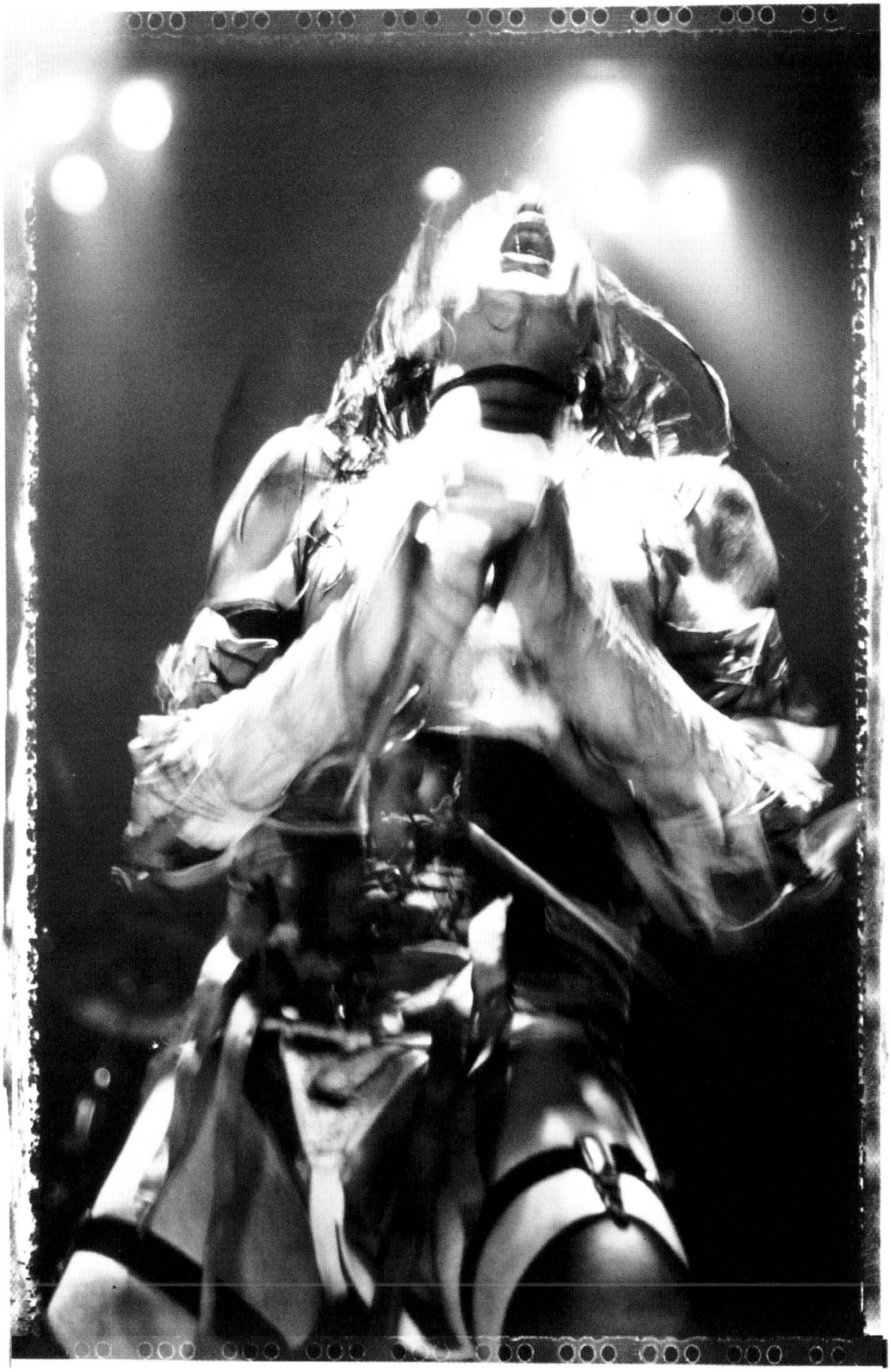

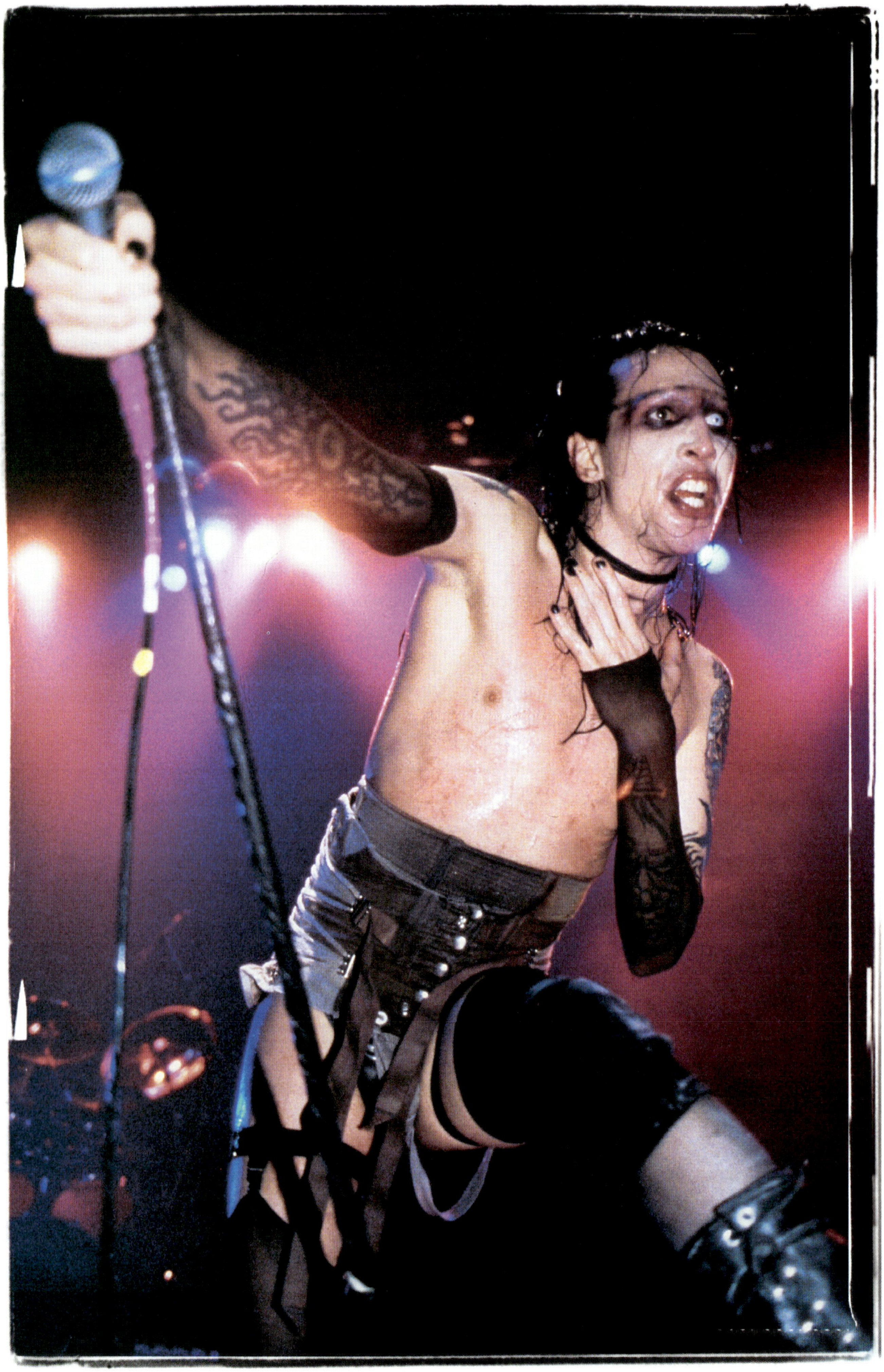

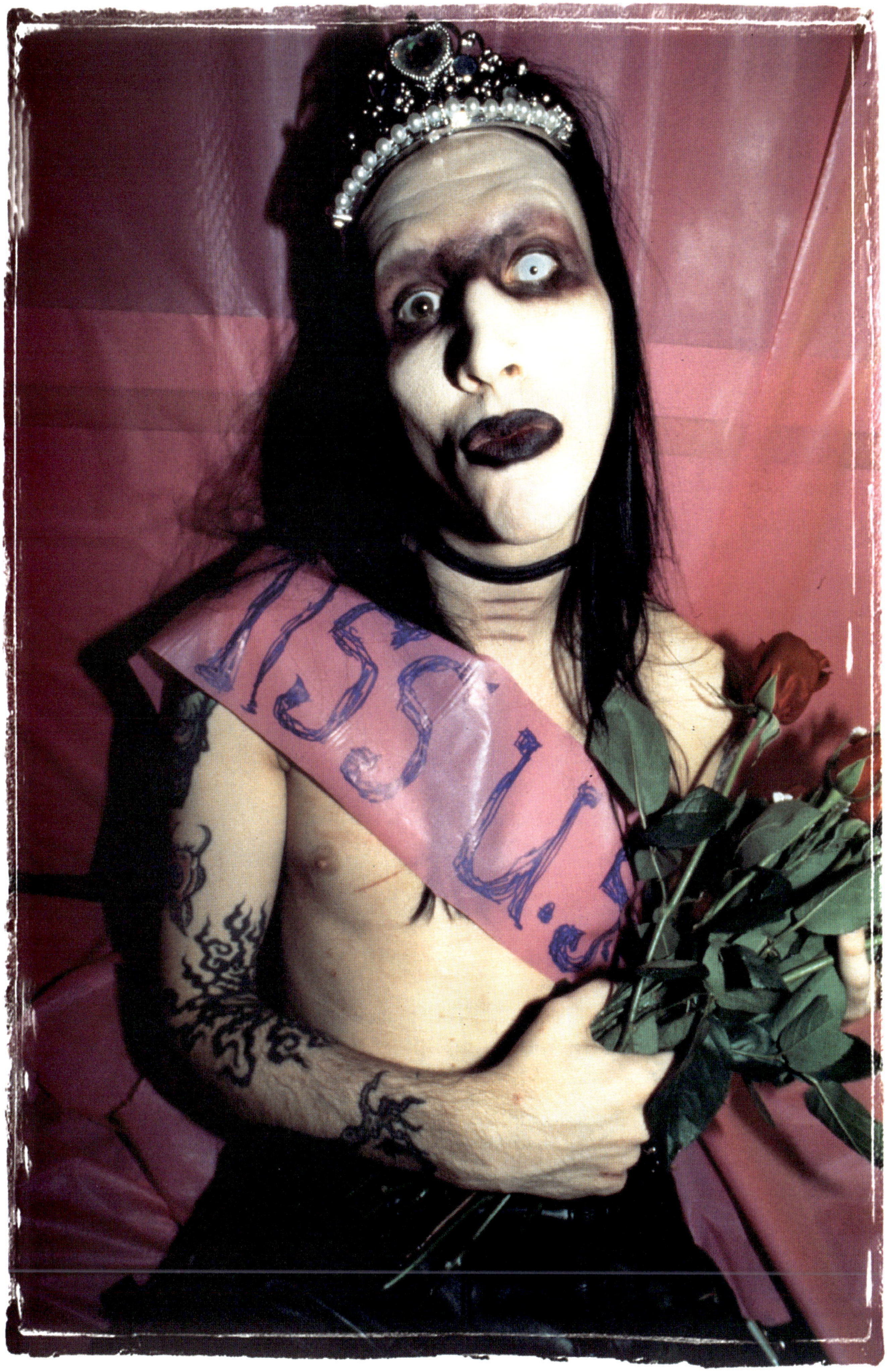

nature stage movements for our hero include bending over backward and forward, hanging onto the mic stand for dear life, and scratching like a dog. Or the outrageous frontman might ceremoniously set a fire in a saucepan on a pedestal and then warm his hands over it like a demented hobo from another planet. To add to the otherworldly atmosphere, Manson gigs often featured a huge Ouija board backdrop, a 666 logo on speakers, a dismembered baby doll hanging from a harness, or an enormous candy cane. But all of this is just background for the band members themselves. Manson's emaciated six-foot-one-inch frame made enough of an impression on its own, but the Reverend saw fit to enhance his image with feet-high stilts and surgical braces. Daisy, ever the most conservative, might sport a Blondie T-shirt with his blue hair and ink-black eyebrows. Twiggy, looking like a doll's worst nightmare, played bass in a green and white housecoat, smeared red lipstick, false eyelashes, and a kid's candy necklace. Pogo decorated his keyboard with what appeared to be goat and human heads. As a final mental image to take home, the audience was often treated to Manson's black vinyl thong bikini for the final encore.

And backstage? After the freak show? Little is known about the band's off-stage activities, although much can be imagined. One bizarre glimpse into the world of Marilyn Manson on the road was afforded by Twiggy, who confessed to *Circus* magazine in their July 15, 1996, issue that "I like to keep the bus clean. I just put on the Bee Gees' Greatest Hits. Not the disco stuff, but the early mod stuff. Pre-'Jive Talking' days. That was one of my pastimes on tour—put that record on and clean the bus with a duster." Well, truth is stranger than fiction. Squeaky-clean behind the scenes, the tour raged on through February 1996, at which point the band pulled back into their own world. And this time only God knew what would emerge from their bubbling cauldron.

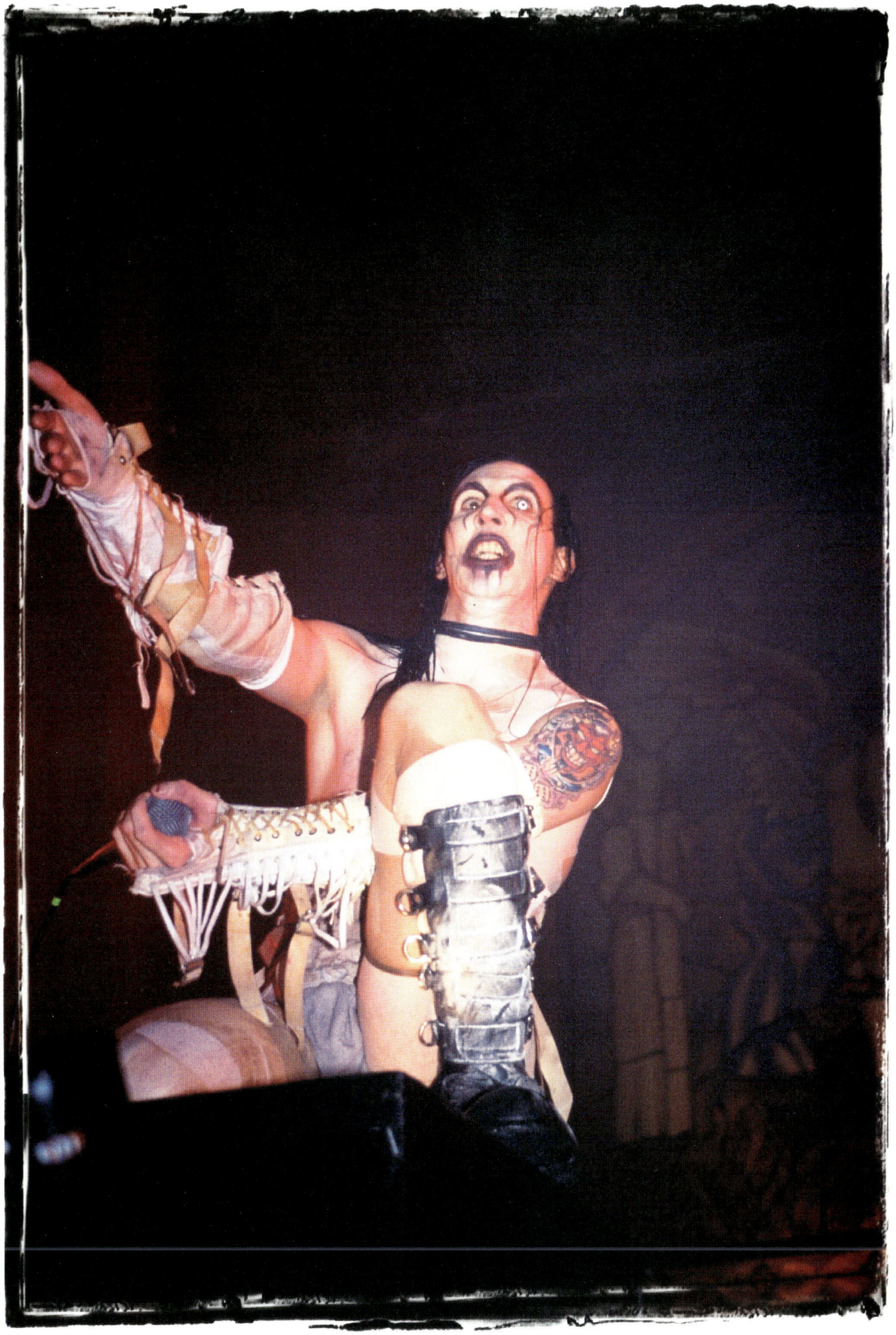

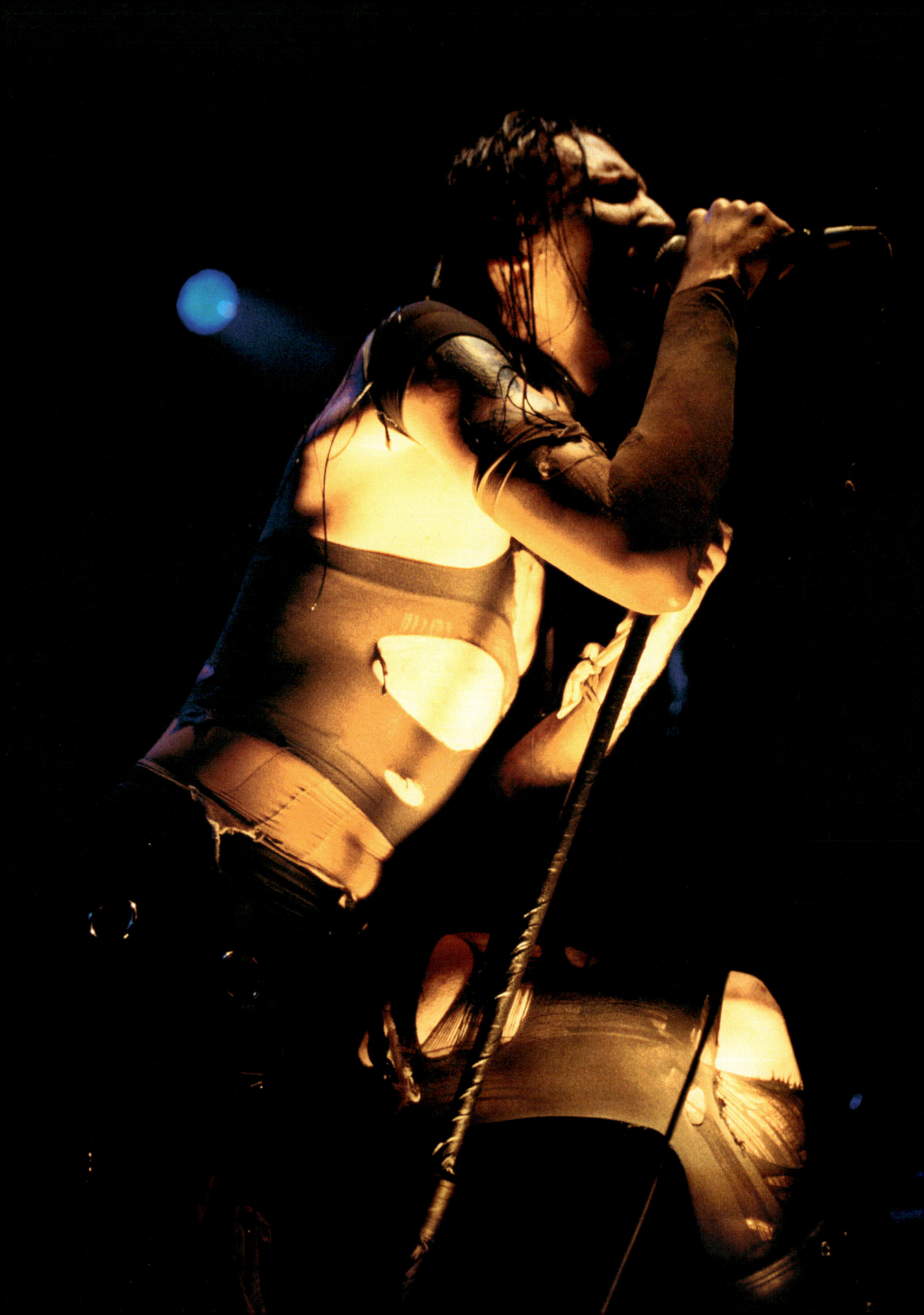

# HELL on EARTH

The only way to go was down. Set to begin work on the album that would scare the life out of the status quo, the band descended upon New Orleans, "the closest place to Hell on earth," according to Manson. Trent Reznor, in his customarily morbid style, had chosen a former funeral home as the site of his new state-of-the-art Nothing Studios. And what better spot for Marilyn Manson's newest, most dangerous experiment to date? The band set out to bring themselves to the brink of insanity, dabbling in near-death experiences and pain endurance rituals, and pushing themselves to musical and mental limits. The outcome, an album brazenly entitled *Antichrist Superstar*, was not reached without sacrifice.

Before the end of the recording venture, Daisy Berkowitz announced that he was leaving the band. Whether it was his unwillingness to go along with the band's desire to experiment musically (and otherwise) on the new album or his reluctance to dive headlong into the Marilyn Manson Land of No Return, Daisy, it seemed, had had enough. "We really tapped into the subconscious-staying up four days in a row, sleep deprivation, all sorts of unmentionable acts of self-torture. These things, I guess, were real alien to Daisy. He wasn't into making life into art. He looked at it more as a job, whereas we embraced life and art as one," Marilyn told *Guitar World* in December 1996. Although he and Berkowitz were the founding members and had made it together through the swamps of Florida to the Grand Canyon–esque brink of fame and, ideally, worldwide domination, the relationship between the two had become increasingly "turbulent." As Manson rationalized, "There's always been an element of friction there—one of those singer/guitar player tension things. But in our case, it never really jelled into a good working dynamic." Manson's official statement on the split explained that the recording of the album was "difficult as it involves many trips dangerously close to chaos. . . . Unfortunately Berkowitz had grown creatively in a different direction, and left the band as we were beginning this project. We wish him success but plan to leave this situation stronger than ever." Daisy's own statement said, "Marilyn Manson have been together for six years and I believe that now the time is right for me to concentrate on my own music and other projects of special interest. I wish the best for Marilyn Manson." He has since been rumored to be working on a new musical venture under the name Three Ton Gate.

Wasting no time, the remaining Manson family put ads out for a new guitarist. Zim Zum, who for all intents and purposes may be a very stylish mute with killer guitar skills, remains a bit of a mystery. The only hardcore evidence that he did not drop from the heavens (or rise from the fiery depths of Hell) when Daisy retired is his documented participation in the Chicago band Life, Sex, and Death. One can't help but wonder if his not having taken the usual Marilyn Manson–esque moniker is an indication of superior or inferior standing as a fledgling. The only clue thus far is Manson's statement to *Circus* magazine that Zim Zum "joined *Antichrist Superstar* more than he joined Marilyn Manson." The name Zim Zum is certainly mysterious, and can be traced to the term for "extraction" in the Hebrew Cabala (God "extracting" himself from space in order to allow Creation to take place). As the Reverend himself put it to *Alternative Press* in February 1997, the name Zim Zum comes from that of "an angel that was created to do God's dirty work in the Old Testament days." Manson insisted that when Zim Zum auditioned, "before he even began playing I felt like he'd be the right guy. I like his confidence and his attitude." Daisy Berkowitz was credited as a writer and guitarist on the new album, with Zim Zum down as "live guitarist for Antichrist Superstar." The fact that he survived the recording sessions alone seems to be an indication that he was meant to be part of the band as they headed toward their new millennium.

The ambience in Nothing Studios must have been bizarre beyond comprehension; Twiggy Ramirez found it worth comment. As he told *Circus* in July 1996, "A lot of the staff is a little weird. A lot of them wear, I don't know if it's a uniform or what, but they wear gray wigs with clip-on ear-

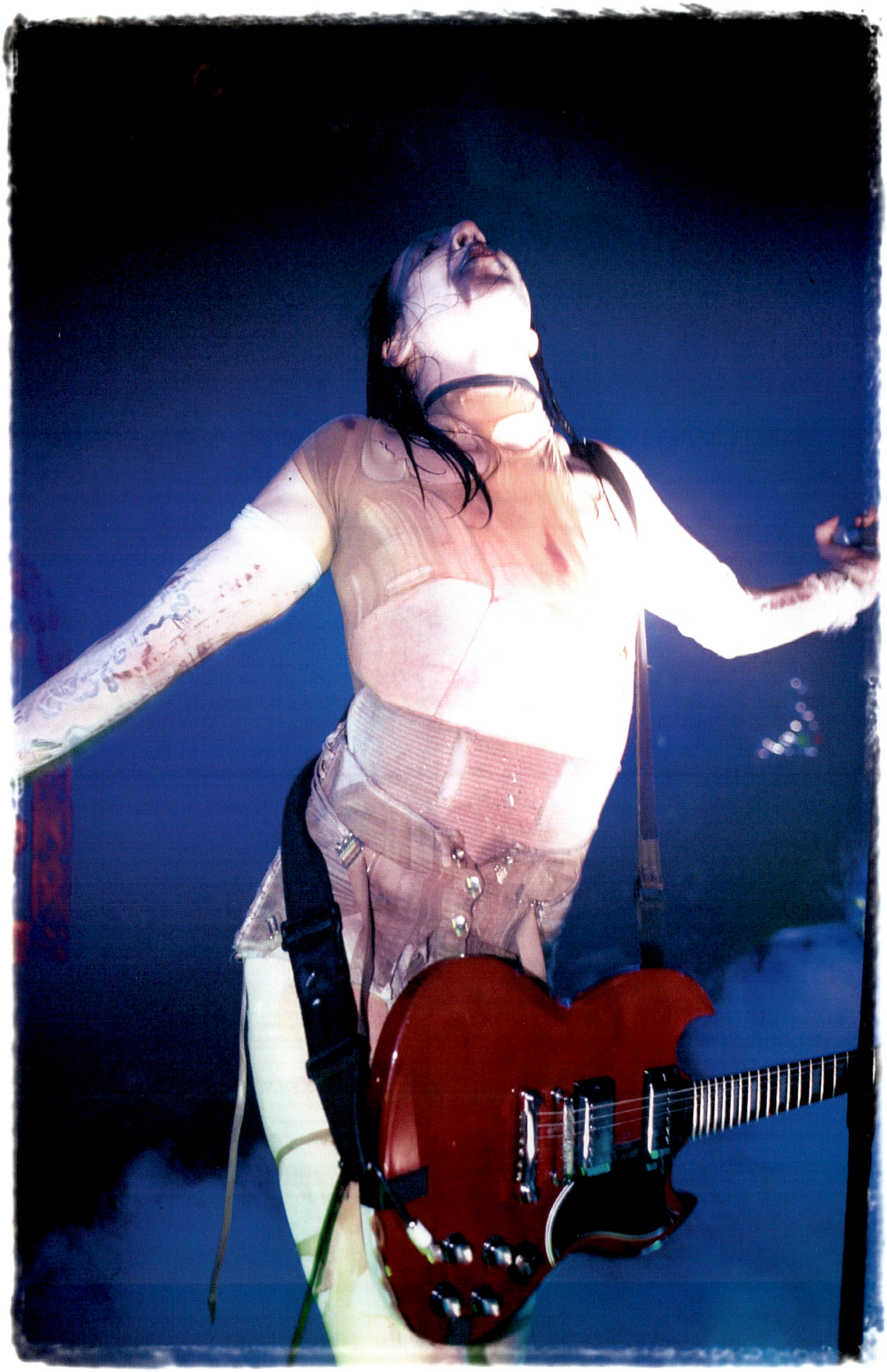

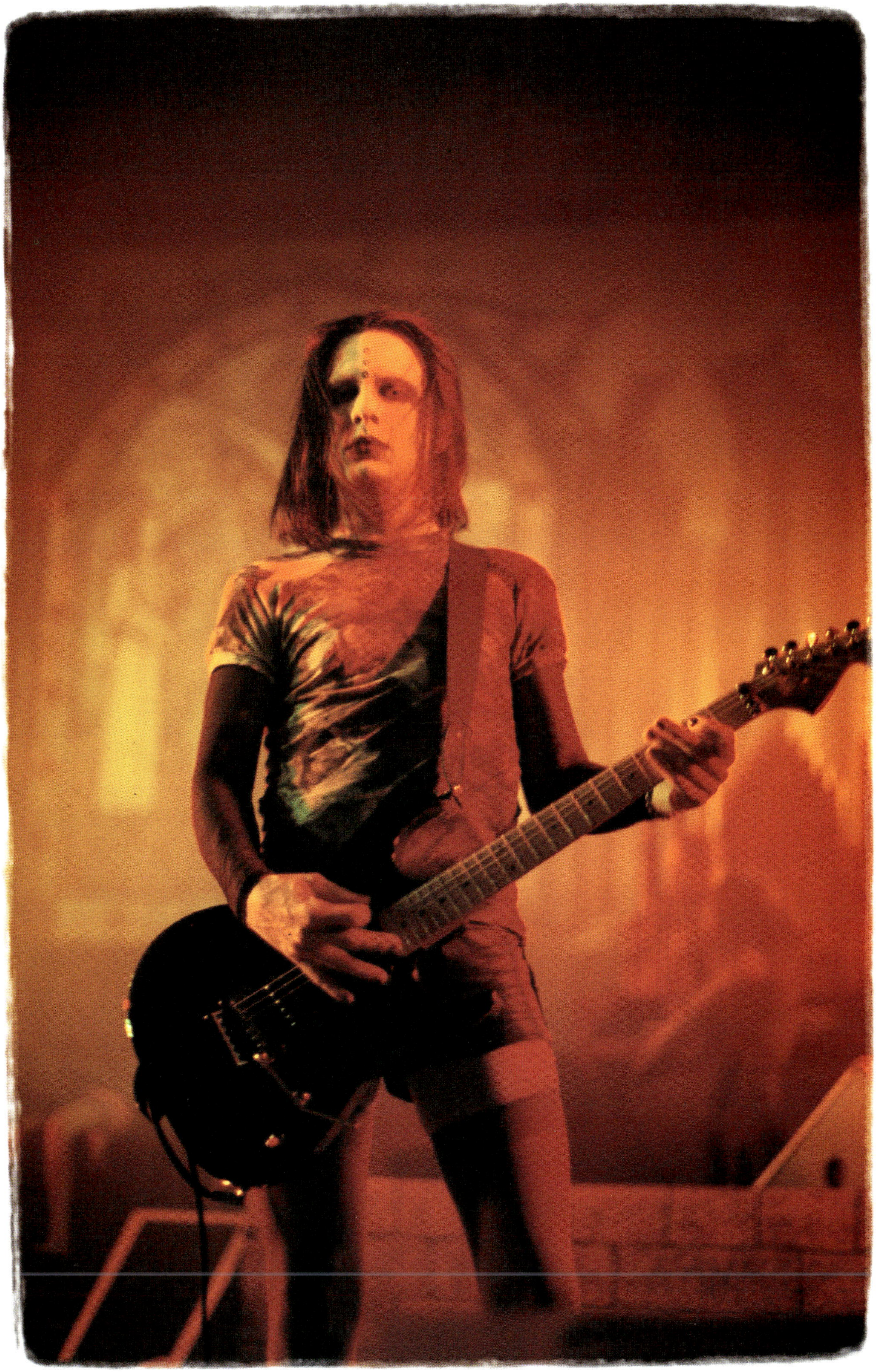

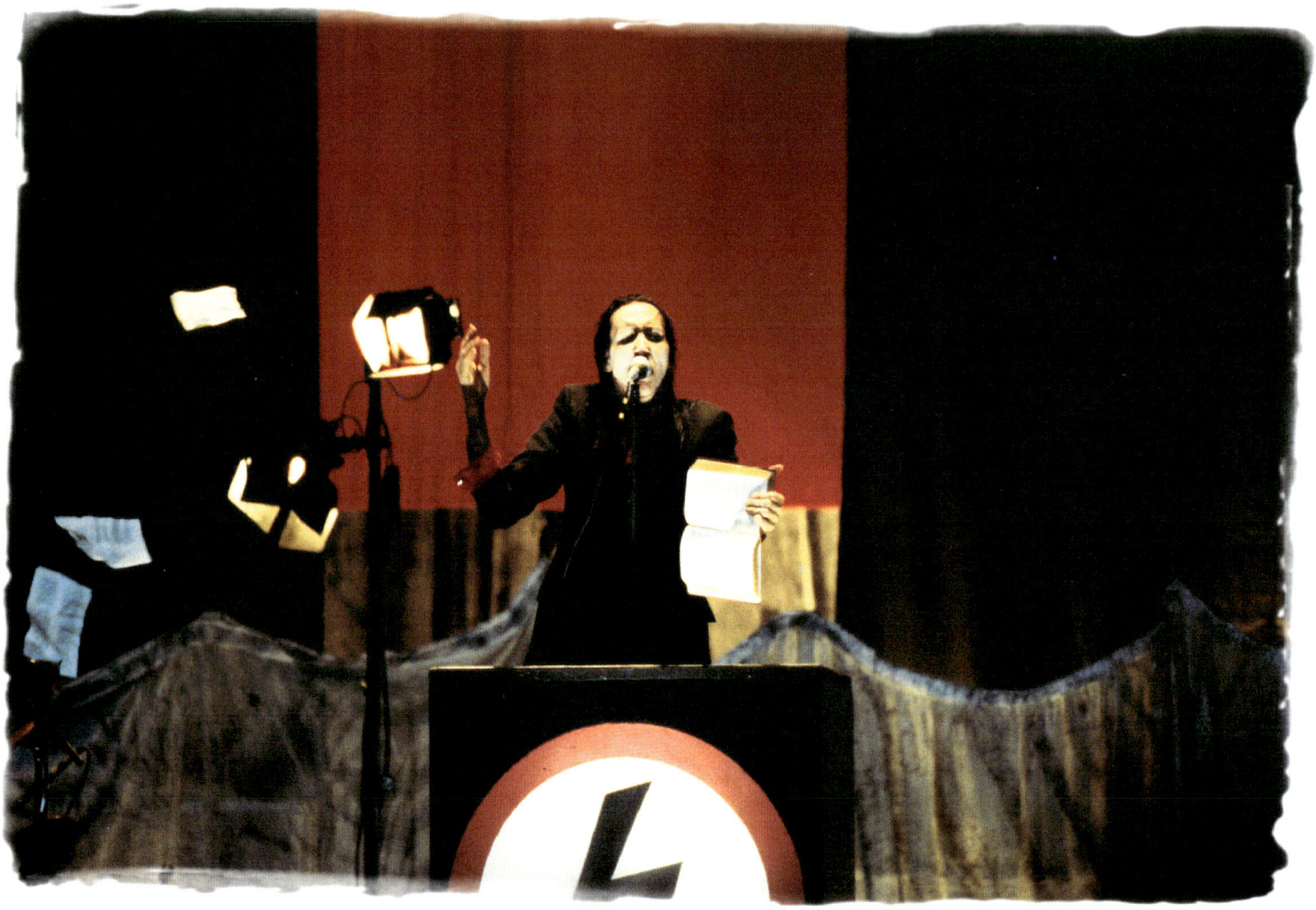

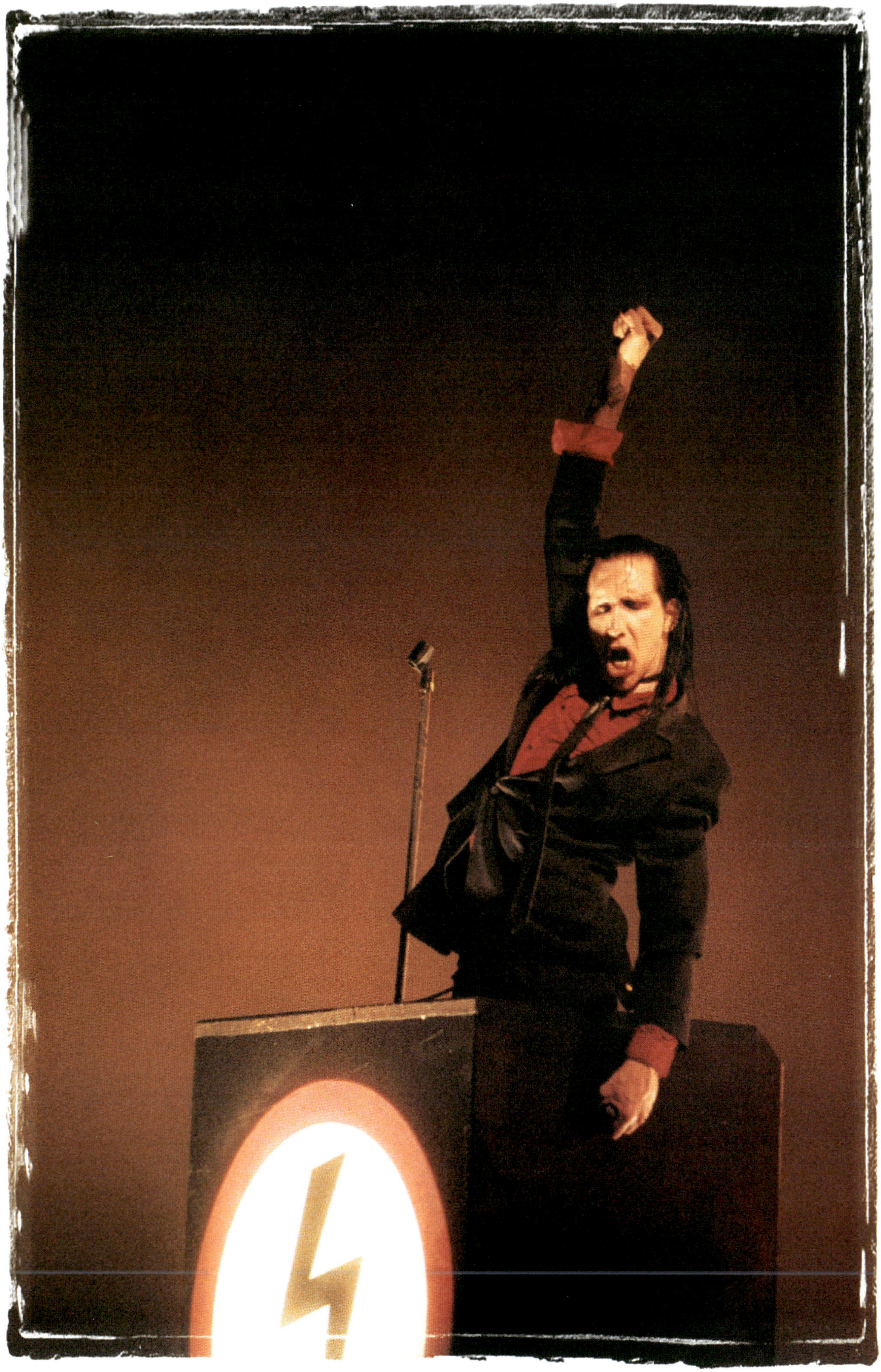

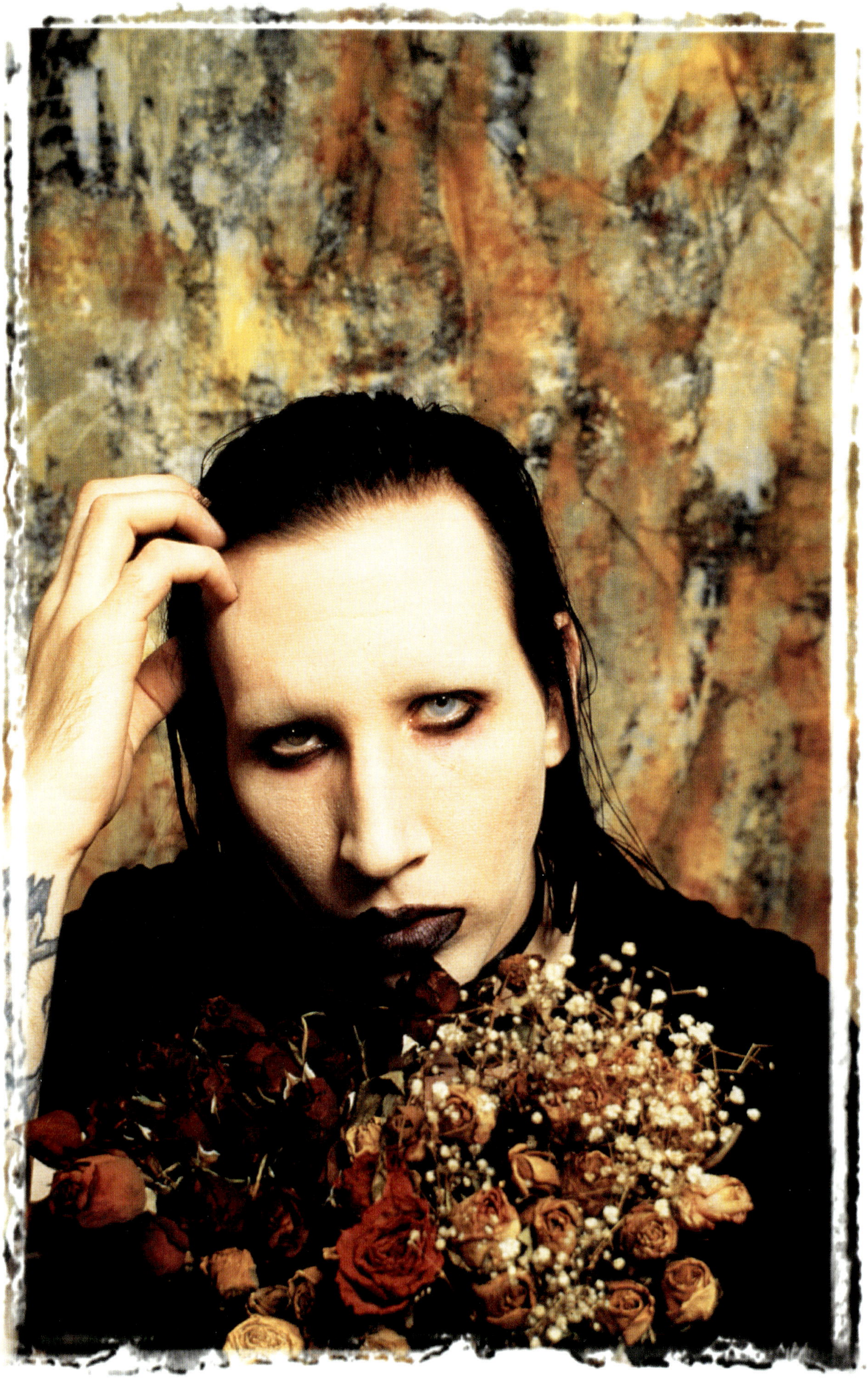

rings. It's a bit odd, but I guess it's part of the atmosphere." Trent himself apparently took to donning a Quiet Riot mask whilst mixing the album. The members of Marilyn Manson added their own touch of madness—aside from the obvious of course—by setting up tents in the middle of the studio, camping out amongst the recording gear like high-tech bedouins.

As for the much-speculated upon influence of drugs on the creation of *Antichrist Superstar*, Manson is characteristically straightforward. He confessed to *Circus* magazine in its June 17, 1997, issue that there was "a seemingly never ending supply of different drugs and pills in New Orleans, and it had a certain influence on the recording process," but stressed that it was more the otherworldly atmosphere of the city that inspired the sessions in the studio, recalling that "the smell of death and decay was everywhere and it certainly crept on the album. That was the most powerful influence ever. It made us realize just how much death is a natural part of life."

The music itself on the new album is a definite departure. Slick, skillful, and ultimately scarier, it presented the fully-realized potential of the Marilyn Manson machine. As Trent Reznor said in *Spin*'s March 1997 issue, "I wanted to show that the band had some scope, that it wasn't all guitar-bass-drums."  Manson told *Guitar World* magazine in December 1996 that "We wanted to go to an outside source like Trent and have him put our vision together." He went on to declare, "We were in a different state of mind when we made that record. So sometimes we're not even sure what we did. It was very stream-of-consciousness." As Twiggy mysteriously put forth to *Circus* in July 1996, *Antichrist Superstar* "was recorded in the future already, and it was sent back. So it's already done, we just have to make it so people can hear it today. Because it's not out yet. It's the future, but it's the past cause it's really all the same. The record from the future, but it's about the past—the past that hasn't happened yet."

*Antichrist Superstar*, released on October 8, 1996, entered the charts at Number Three, finding itself in the unlikely company of Number One and Two acts Celine Dion and Kenny G. The sudden juxtaposition of an outfit led by a man *Guitar World* magazine called "profoundly ugly and violently disturbed" with the wholesome, soap and water goodness of the current God and Goddess of middle-of-the-road musical values caused the mainstream media to sit up and listen. Or, at least, give the freaks a cursory mention. *Entertainment Weekly*, in its October 25, 1996, edition, spotlighted the album in its Charts section, scoffing, "Antichrists, maybe; superstars, not yet," and went on to reassure their readers that the album, which they described as Manson's "latest lurid attempt to capture the hearts, minds, and school lunch money of young America," would surely drop off the charts none too soon. The only problem was that the album, which sold 132,000 copies in its first week, was actually quite good. *Rolling Stone* featured *Antichrist Superstar*—along with a ghoulish cartoon of a worm with the Reverend Manson's head winding its way through a garden of skulls and bones—in its November 28, 1996, "New Recordings" section. Awarding a respectable three and a half stars, the venerable music mag declared that the album "could make the group rock's next billion dollar babies."

The sixteen songs on the album tell the story of a worm that metamorphoses into an angel. They are divided into three segments, "Cycle I: The Heirophant," "Cycle II: Inauguration of the Worm," and "Cycle III: Disintegration Rising." These songs present an older, darker, and more serious Marilyn Manson; one whose threat to take over the world had itself undergone a metamorphosis from childlike taunt to alarming promise. Opening with the line, "I am so all-American, I'd sell you suicide," in the track "Irresponsible Hate Anthem," the album is a relentless seventy-seven minute rampage whose quieter moments are even more ominous than its screams of terror. As Manson told *Spin*, "This record is about personal strength and by seeing my own death and learning from it is where I obtain that strength."

Manson explores his own subconscious through touching upon his own experiences. The song "Kinderfeld" was inspired by his grandfather—a truck driver who, according

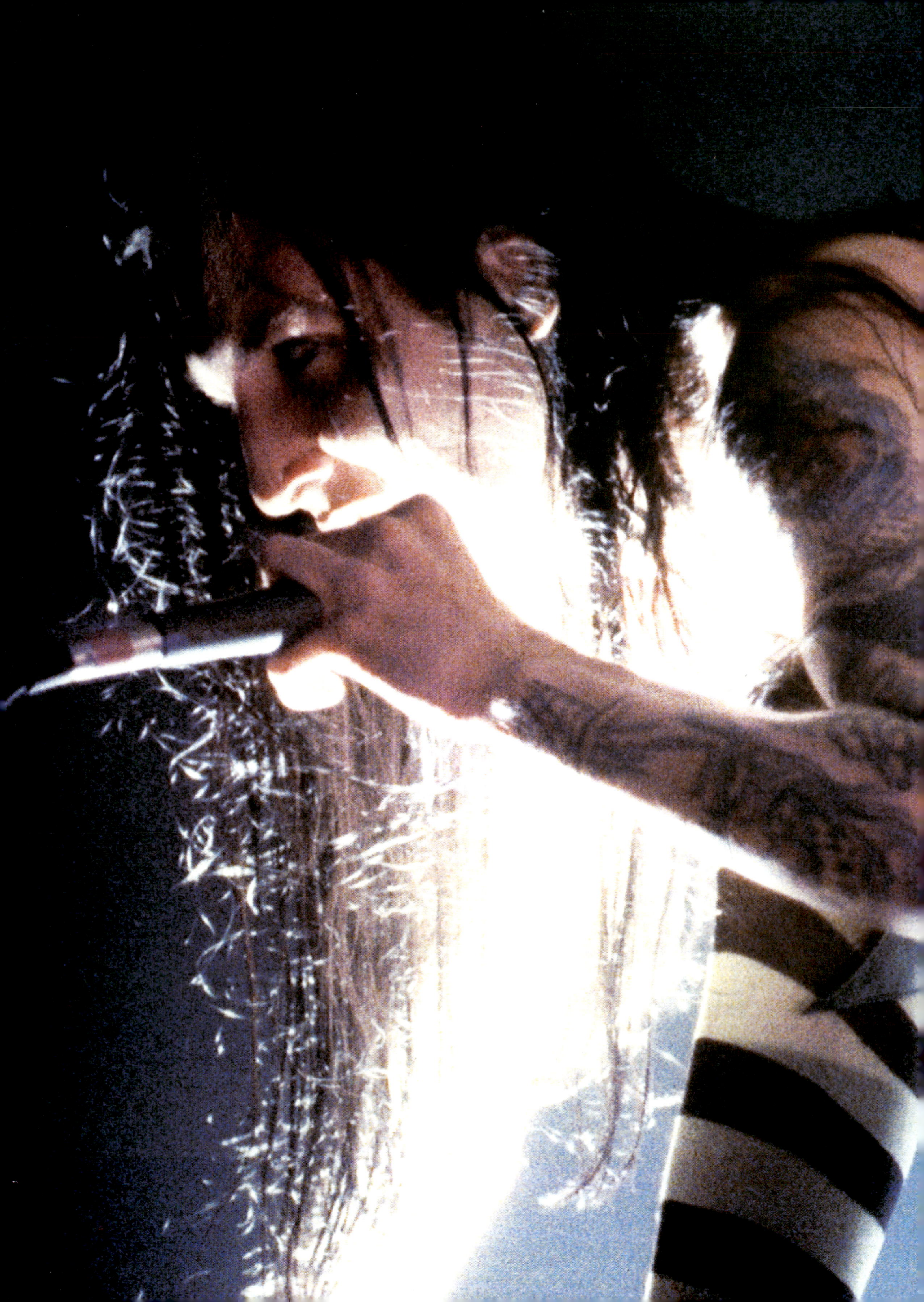

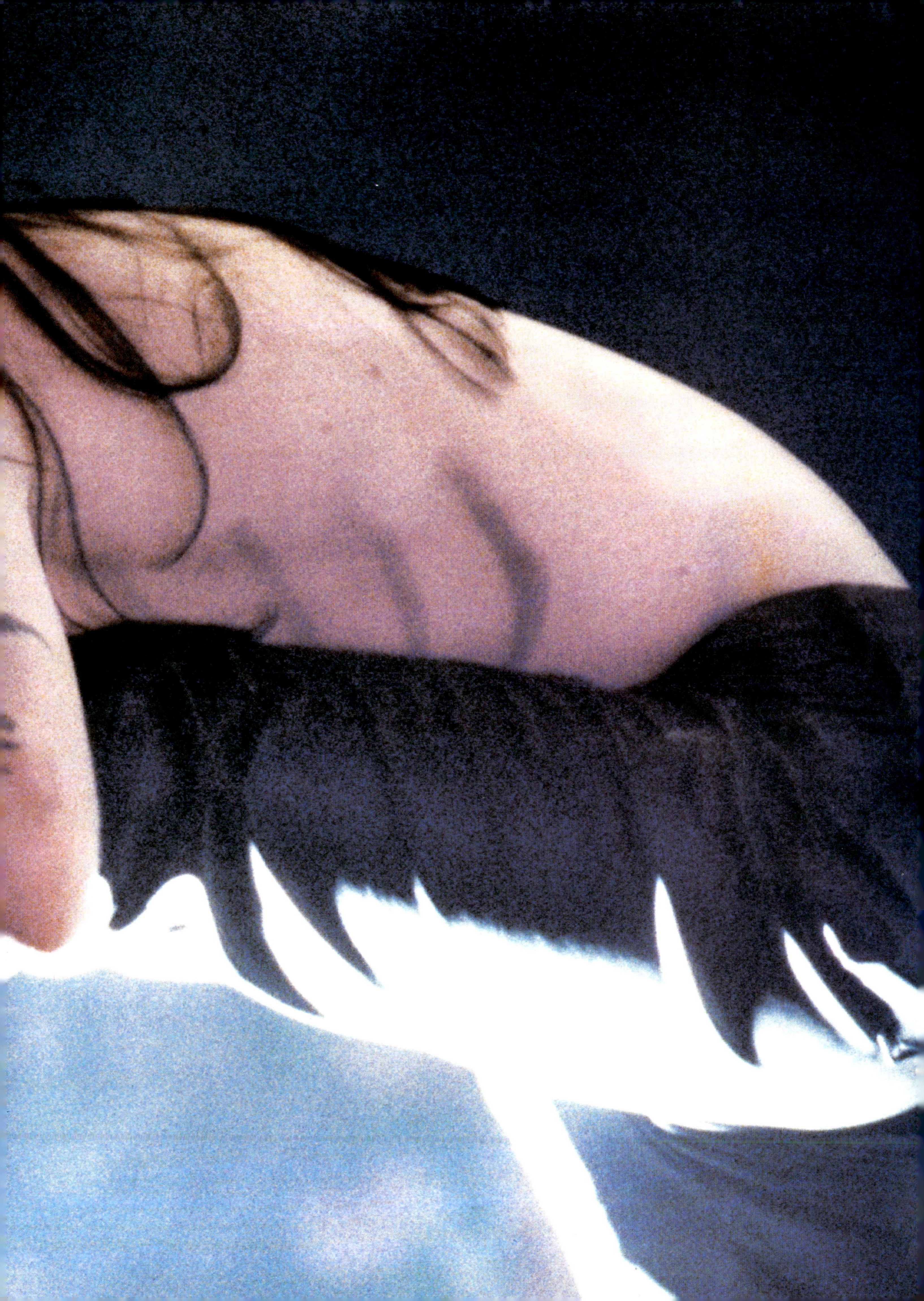

to family myth, was caught out upon arrival at the hospital after an accident wearing women's lingerie under his clothes—who used to masturbate while running his train set in the basement. Manson, who admitted to *Q* magazine that "just thinking about it gives me a chill," described his most recent visit to his grandmother, who still lives in the house she shared with his now-deceased grandfather, when he ventured down the basement stairs to find that "the train set was still there and there were all these rusty paint cans hanging from the ceiling. I opened them and they're still filled with 16mm porno movies." "Tourniquet" ("She's made of hair and bone and little teeth/And things I cannot speak") recounts his recurring dream of creating a companion for himself out of the his own hair and baby teeth combined with prosthetic limbs.

The album's first single, "The Beautiful People," pounded its way onto the airwaves. Manson's voice, as frightening in falsetto as in its customary hoarse howl, bombarded mainstream society and music to the beat of tribal-techno drums, putting down the so-called beautiful ones in one foul blow. The accusational cries of "Hey You, what do you see?/Something beautiful, something free?" were soon on high-rotation MTV courtesy of a gorgeously disturbing video. It was directed by Floria Sigismondi, the Italian director who is becoming known for visually presenting the dark side of the human mind. Sigismondi has also worked with the likes of Tricky and David Bowie. She told MTV News that "a lot of my images come from that time when you just go to sleep, and I usually end up writing in the dark or just when I wake up," adding, "I think it could get pretty scary if people hide that side of them, and then kind of let it out in other ways, where I'm very visible with it, and it's a safe way." Manson himself, the main inspiration behind the videos disturbing images, told MTV that he introduced Sigismondi to his fondness for "prosthetics and other medical fetishes" and that the band "all went wild with, you know, her ideas. And I think she did a great job. It did leave some bad cuts in my mouth, which unfortunately probably will never heal."

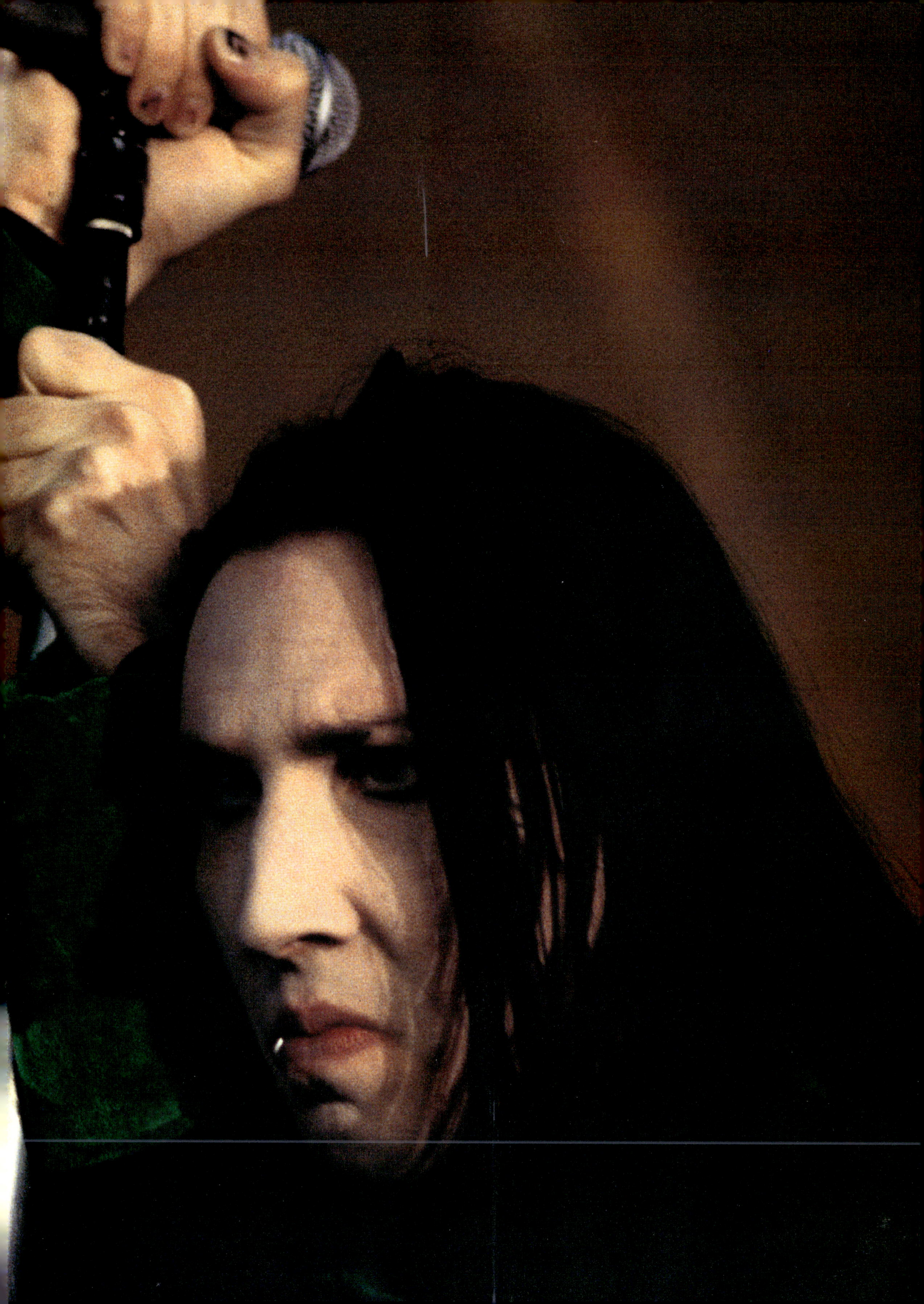

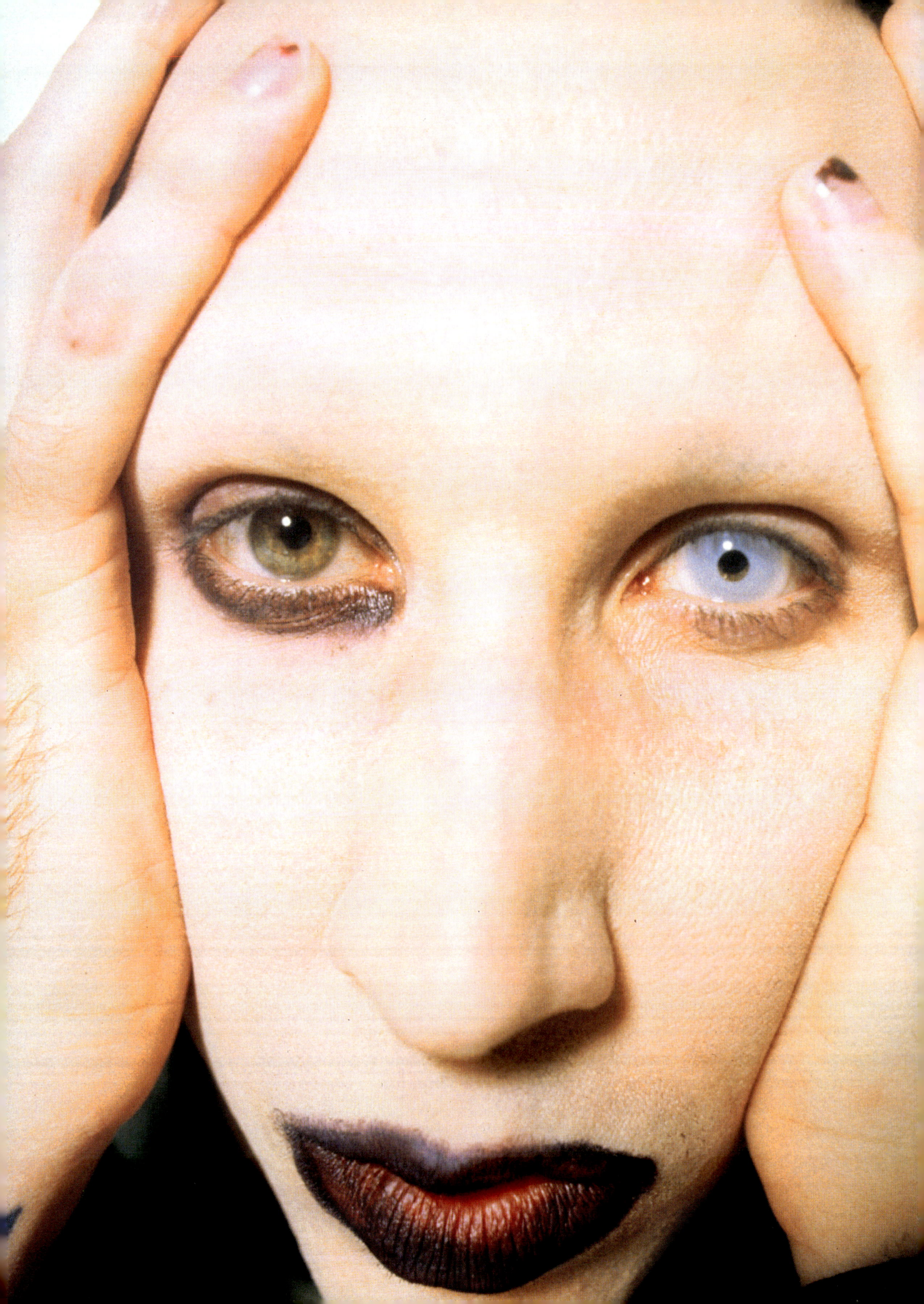

# CONTROVERSY RISING

The shit hit the fan not long after *Antichrist Superstar* hit the stores. Anti–Marilyn Manson sentiments were nothing new, of course. Back in the good old days, the British church and state reportedly hoisted a campaign to ban *Portrait of an American Family* - "[British Member of Parliament] Blackburn, who is also a member of the Church of England Synod," according to the September 24, 1994 edition of the *Daily Insider*, "thinks 'It's appalling. I would ban this sort of thing tomorrow. It's breaking up society.'" But that was smalltime dissension compared to the uproar that broke out and grew to monstrous proportions by the time Marilyn Manson's "Dead to the World" tour began burning its path across America.

*Antichrist Superstar* was barely stocked on the shelves when Senator Joe Lieberman of Connecticut denounced local record stores for "marketing death and degradation as a twisted form of holiday cheer." Lieberman, along with "culture warriors" William Bennett of Empower America and others, confronted none other than the C.E.O. of Seagram for, according to Christopher Stern reporting for Reuters News Service on December 10, 1996, "failing to honor a promise not to distribute music with violent and profane lyrics through his MCA Music Group." Bennett reportedly held up for example the cover of the *Antichrist Superstar* CD and declared it "crap and filth." Empower America and other such ultraconservative organizations have been known to praise retail chain Wal-Mart for refusing to carry CDs of which they do not approve or for carrying them only if the cover artwork and/or lyrics are changed and special edition CDs are manufactured solely for their stores. The attack against record labels for releasing artists' music (whatever next?) and against stores that sell music, for, well, selling music, was to become a full-on battle waged even in cyberspace. The American Family Association announced on its web page that it was "endorsing a nationwide boycott of the Minneapolis-based Best Buy Company because of its sponsorship of the 'Ozzfest' tour which features hate-rock group Marilyn Manson" and issued a press release on June 20, 1997, in which Tim Wildmon, Vice President of the A.F.A., is quoted as saying, "Best Buy's promotion of this hateful act is the moral equivalent of dealing drugs to children."

The "Dead to the World" tour 1996–97 kicked off on October 3, 1996, in Kalamazoo, Michigan, at the State Theatre. And once the show was underway, there was no stopping the madness. Marilyn Manson, the band and the man, were to take on much more than just another tour. The Antichrist Superstar was to find himself up against the Religious Right, and it wasn't going to be pretty. He was attempting to play by his rules on their turf, and when the Manson tour bus pulled into the Heartland's hometowns, that famed Southern hospitality took on a decidedly unwelcoming attitude. To say the least.

Marilyn Manson, perhaps wisely, stuck to the apparently more sympathetic North at the start of the tour, playing in Illinois, Ohio, New York, Canada, Massachusetts, Rhode Island, New Jersey (the October 31 gig which proved uneventful save a bomb threat or two and rumors of Mr. Manson's planned Halloween celebratory suicide), and Washington, D.C. The band then slipped down to the relative safety and ensured welcome of its "home state" of Florida before skipping town and leaving the good old U.S.A. to head over to Santiago, Chili, for the November 22 Close-Up Festival to play in the prestigious company of Bad Religion, Cypress Hill, and the Sex Pistols. Concerts in Sweden, Denmark, Germany, Belgium, France, Spain, and the UK followed with the band Fluffy as opening act. It was when the former Spooky Kids re-entered America with Drill and L7 as support that the simmering stew of controversy began to boil over. Oklahoma City governor Frank Keating, who MTV News described as "surprisingly knowledgeable" about "the tragically misunderstood Marilyn Manson," declared, in the face of the impending February 5, 1997 gig at the state fairgrounds, that the band is "clearly bent on degrading women, religion, and decency."

The beginning of March gave the clamoring American masses a breather again while the band's traveling show

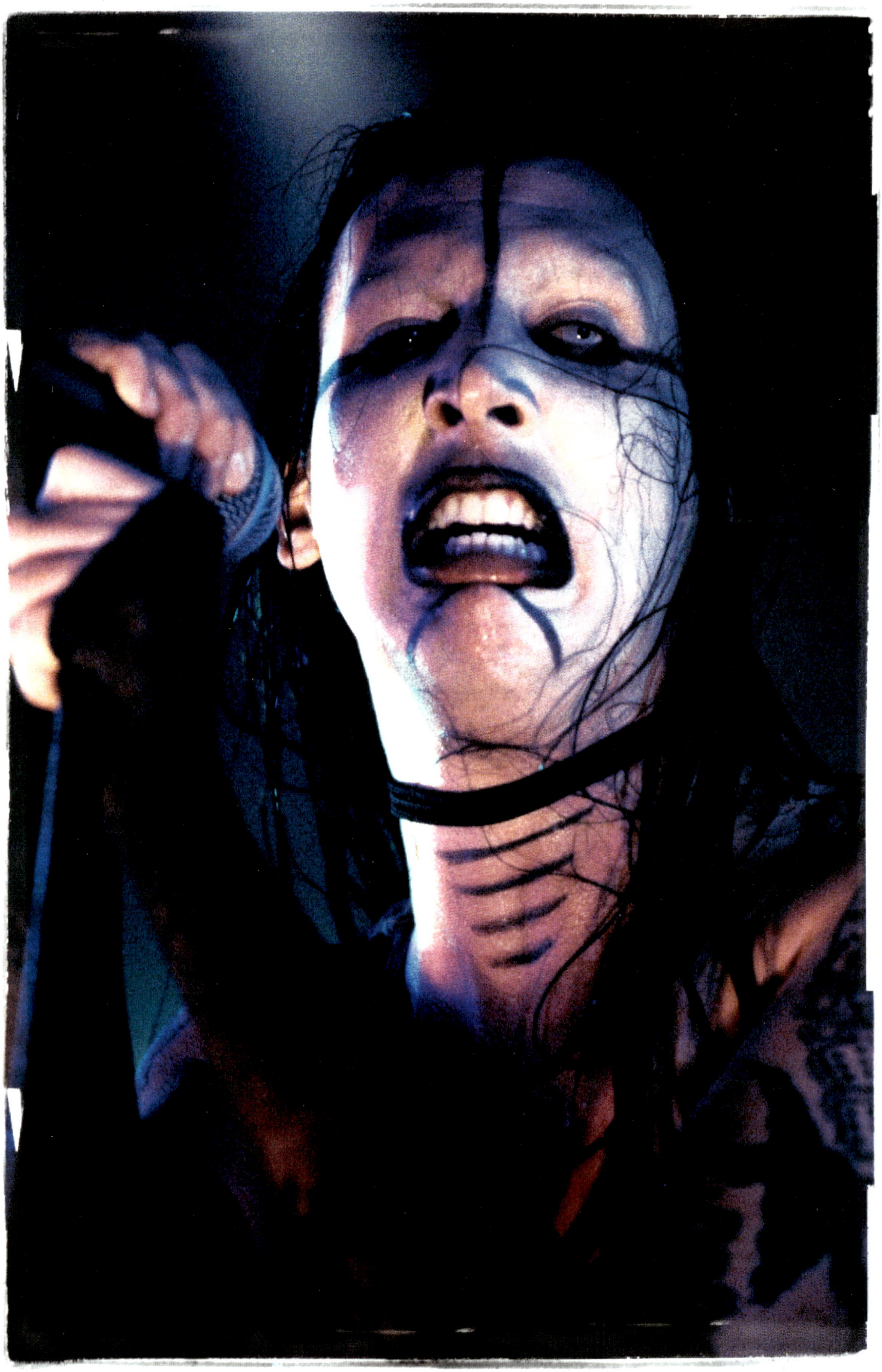

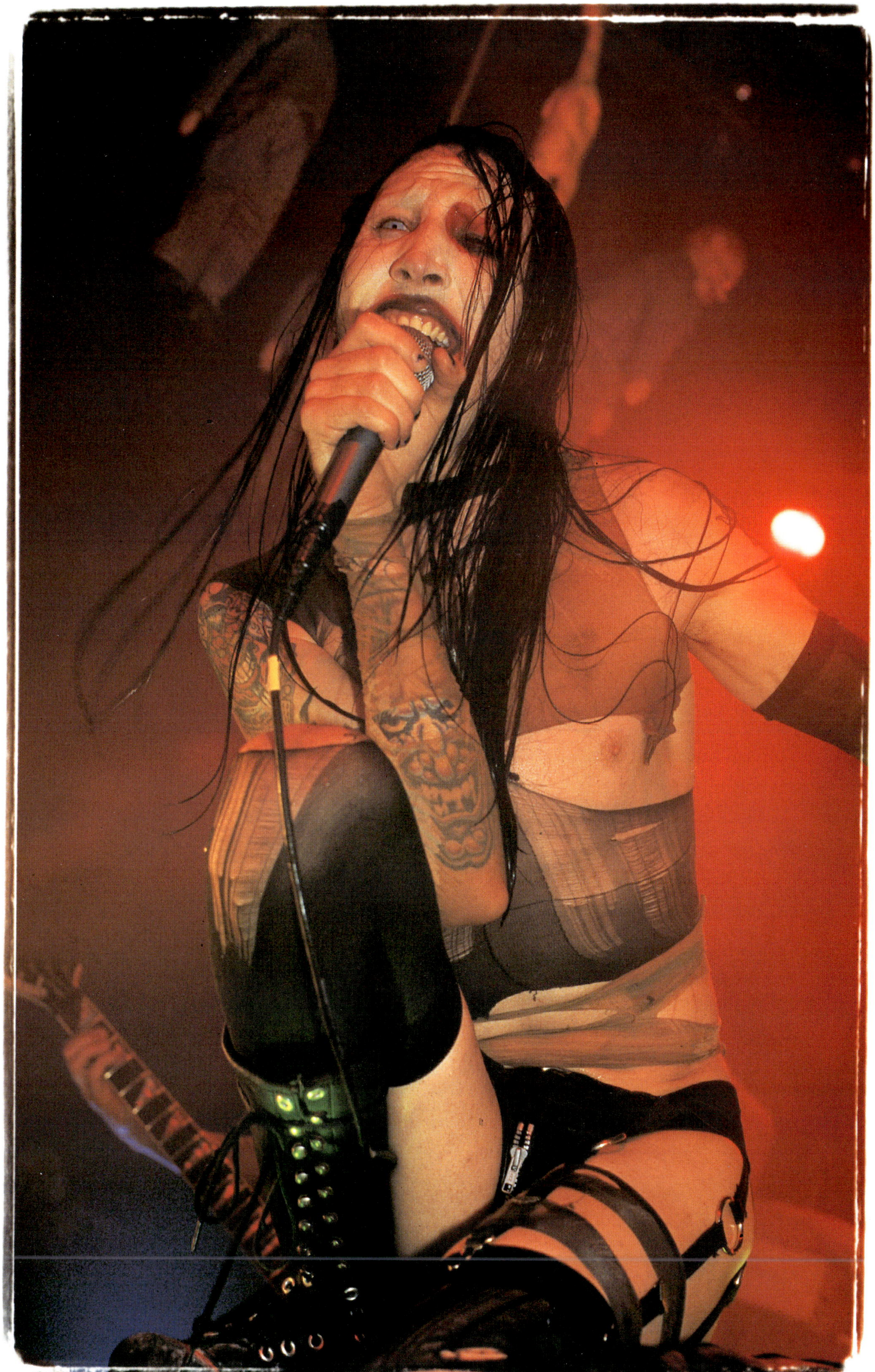

popped over to Japan and then down to Australia and New Zealand. Mr. Manson, in good form, re-entered the States with a bang, tripping onstage in Honolulu, Hawaii, on March 22, landing on a sharp object (try falling on a Manson stage and not hitting something potentially harmful), and cutting an artery in his hand. He was rushed off to the emergency room for stitches. The incident was reported in *Billboard* magazine, which noted that "the accident apparently was not part of the show." Manson's manager reportedly "called MTV News to stress that contrary to local press reports, Marilyn did not slash his wrists intentionally during the show." Who else would, due to a horrible accident, almost die and generate immediate public opinion that the near-tragedy was in fact deliberate?

The next leg of the tour, with New York Loose, Helmet, and Rasputina (a group made up of three female cellists) as support, began on April 5 in LaCrosse, Wisconsin. Oh, and what a fuss! Glenn Walinski, director of the LaCross Center, told none other than *Rolling Stone* (June 12, 1997 issue) that the Manson concert "was the worst thing I've been through. It divided our community." The band then moved on to bring their crusade against all that is run-of-the-mill to a town called Normal, Illinois (whether it remains so is yet to be seen). Protestors turned out with bells on to show their disapproval of the April 17 concert in Jacksonville, Florida. The Associated Press released a statement from a resident of the town; a Stan Carter asserted that the rock star was "pressing hatred and dislike and violence toward Christians. This man is a slap in the face. He's no less an affront than Nazis marching down Myrtle Avenue."

The April 20 concert at the University of South Carolina Coliseum set a precedent by actually being canceled. Unable to handle the pressure "reportedly launched by state treasurer Richard Eckstrom, who first learned about the band at a church service," according to MTV News, the college and promoter Cellar Door Productions decided to call off the festivities, and came to an agreement with the band whereby Marilyn Manson would be paid the reported tidy sum of $40,000 *not* to play! A bill attempting to bar Marilyn Manson from ever performing in a state facility was also introduced by state legislators. As *Rolling Stone* reported in their on-line "Random Notes Daily" on April 14, Eckstrom felt the band was "needlessly offensive and dehumanizing." In a curiously unclear attempt to set forth the state's reasoning behind its anti-Manson stance, Treasury spokesperson Scott Malyerck was quoted as saying, "This group certainly isn't like Olivia Newton-John or Blondie, and is far afield of decent music. . . . We don't think they provide any redeeming qualities whatsoever—social, moral, or musical. And I'm a rock fan." Well, that goes without saying. What the state of the music entertainment industry would be if the main criteria for live performance was similarity to either Olivia Newton-John or Blondie (why these two artists, whose only common attribute is femaleness, have been linked in this context is not immediately evident) is difficult to speculate, but everyone is entitled to their opinion. Except, apparently, Marilyn Manson fans. Mr. Manson's response to all this? He asked MTV, "What do you expect from a state that still flies the Confederate flag?" and succinctly labeled his detractors "fascist bigots."

A Reverend Dana Wilson of Michigan not only attempted to persuade concert promoters to cancel the April 25 Wendler Arena show, but, failing to do so, went for second-best and, with a petition signed by 20,000 locals, put forth his suggestion that concert-goers under eighteen years of age not be allowed to attend the show without a parental chaperon (a concept the Reverend Manson would no doubt greet with glee).

On more than one occasion gigs were canceled due to local protestors' pressure and swiftly rescheduled in the face of ultimately more threatening legal pressure. Despite allegations that the band was "not consistent with our community standards" by Richmond, Virginia, City Manager Robert C. Bobb (a statement in itself inconsistent as some 2,000 tickets had already been sold, presumably to members of said community), the city decided that nasty old Marilyn Manson wasn't all that bad after all and reslated the previously nixed May 10 show. *Billboard*

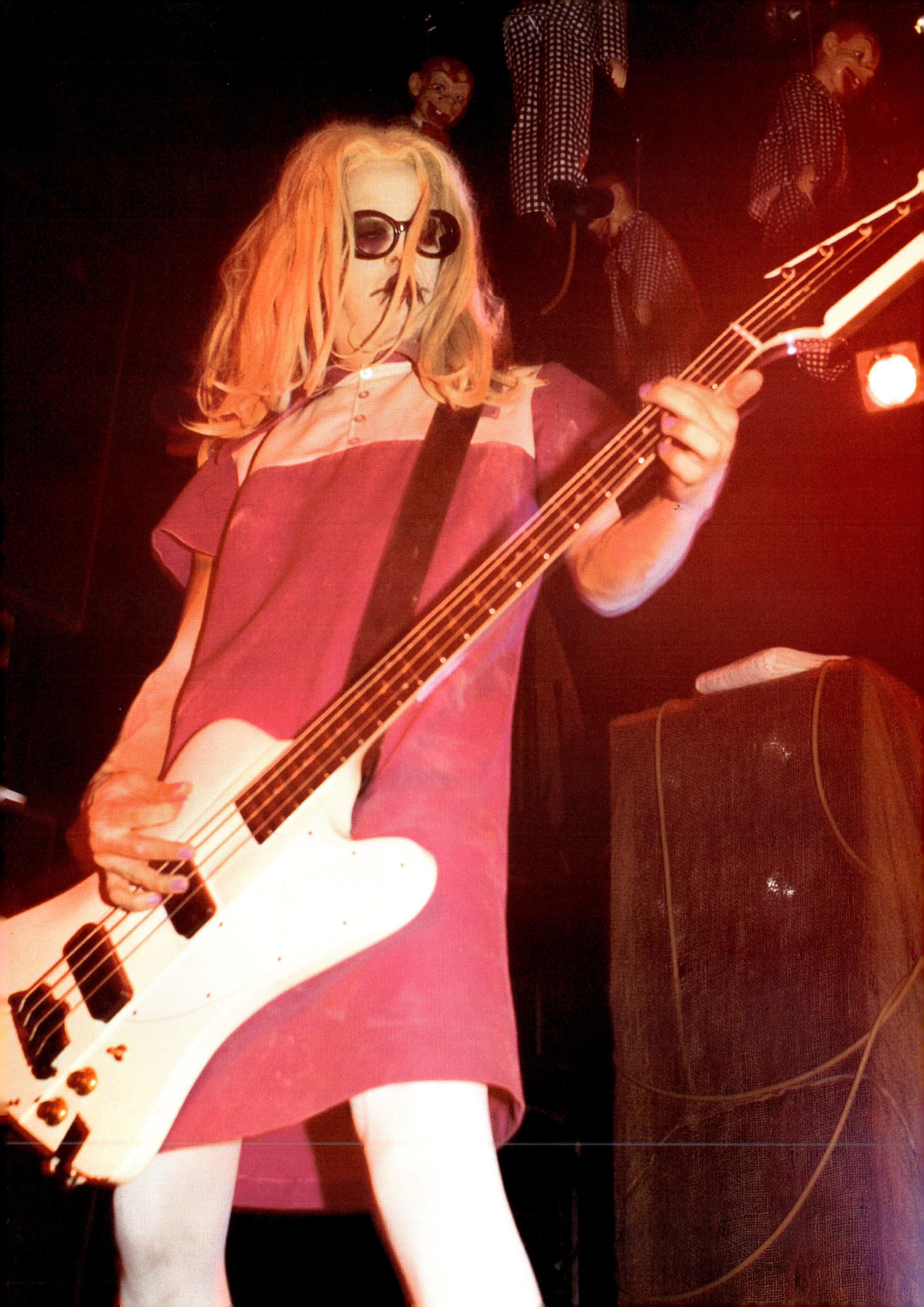

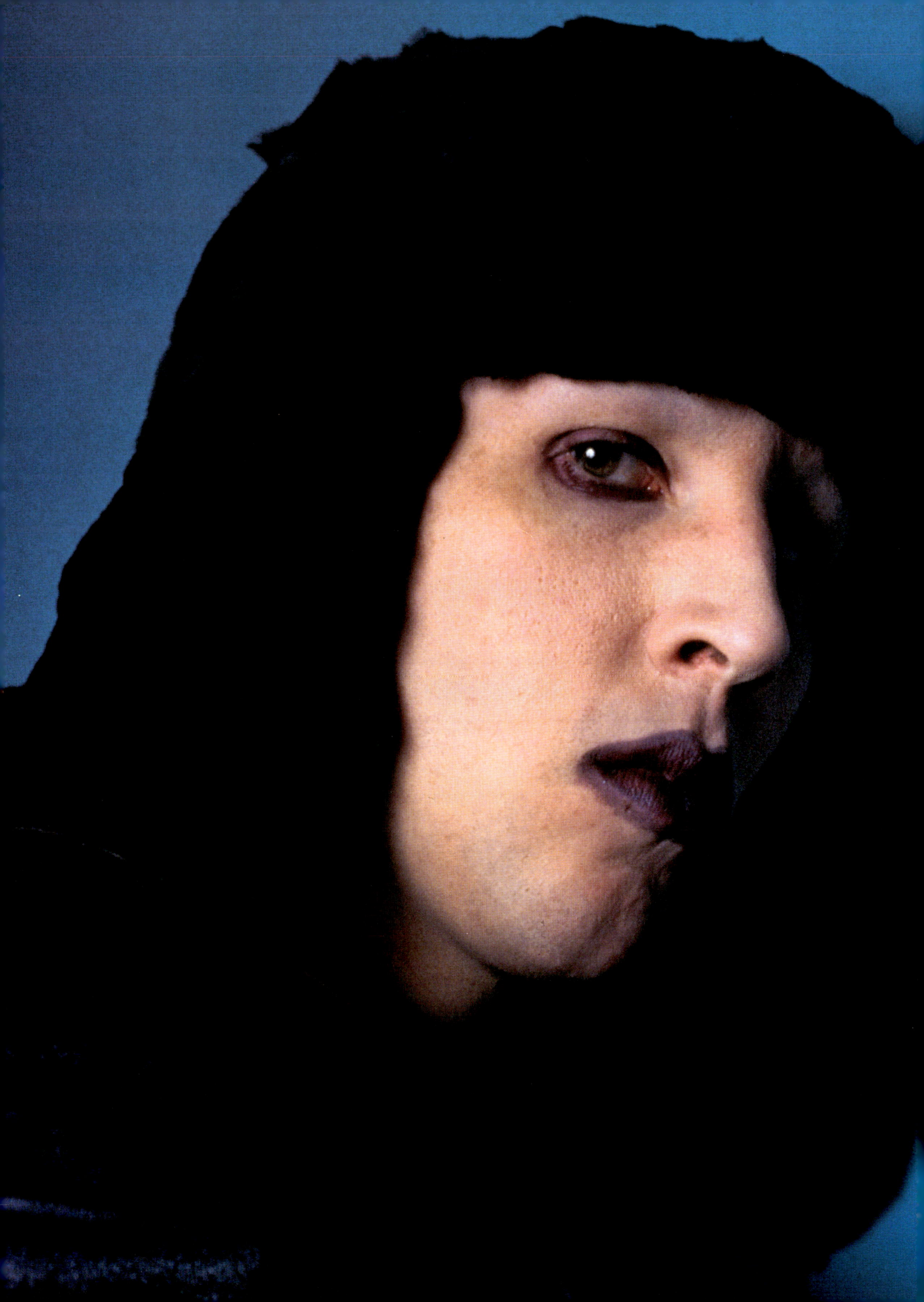

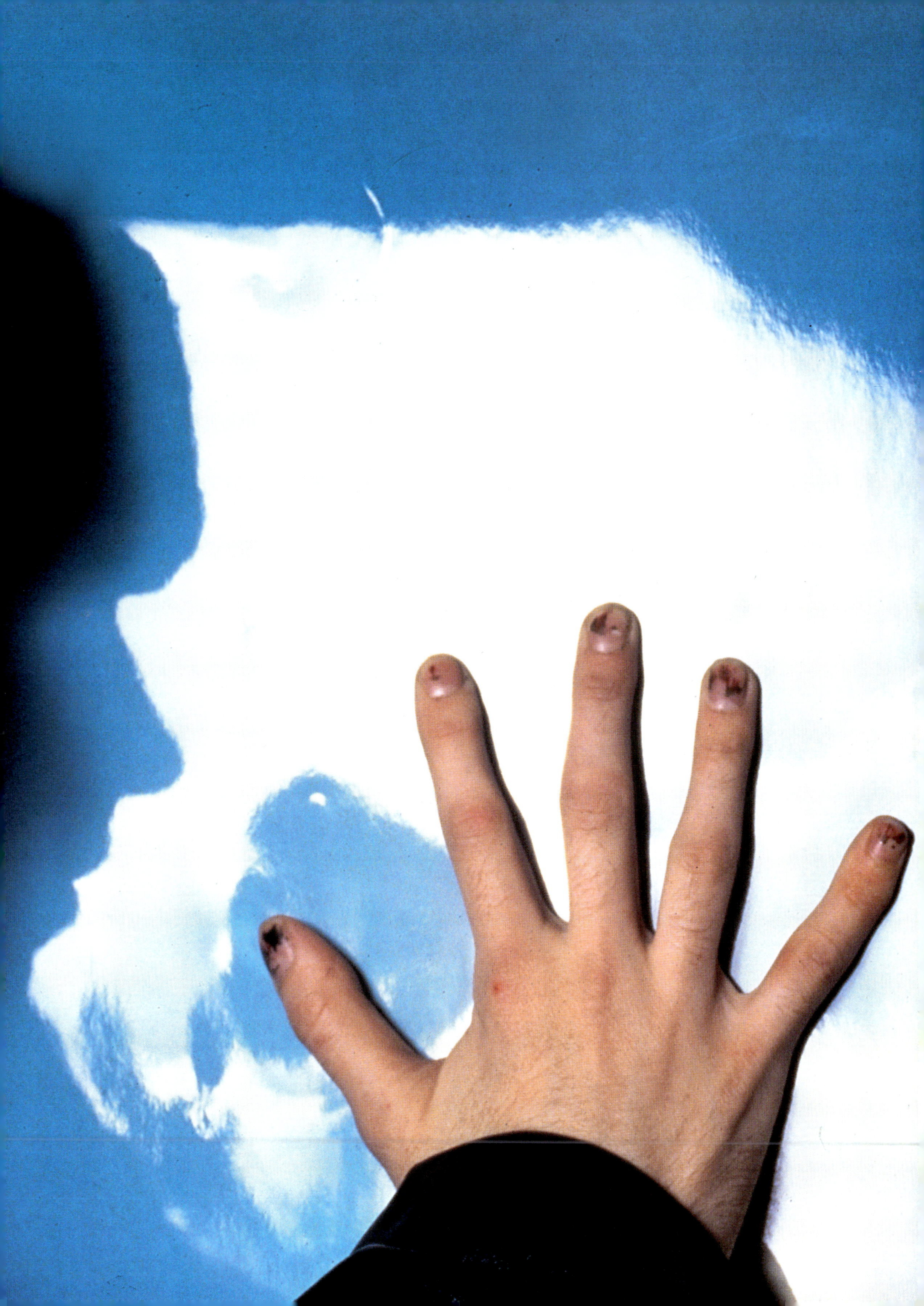

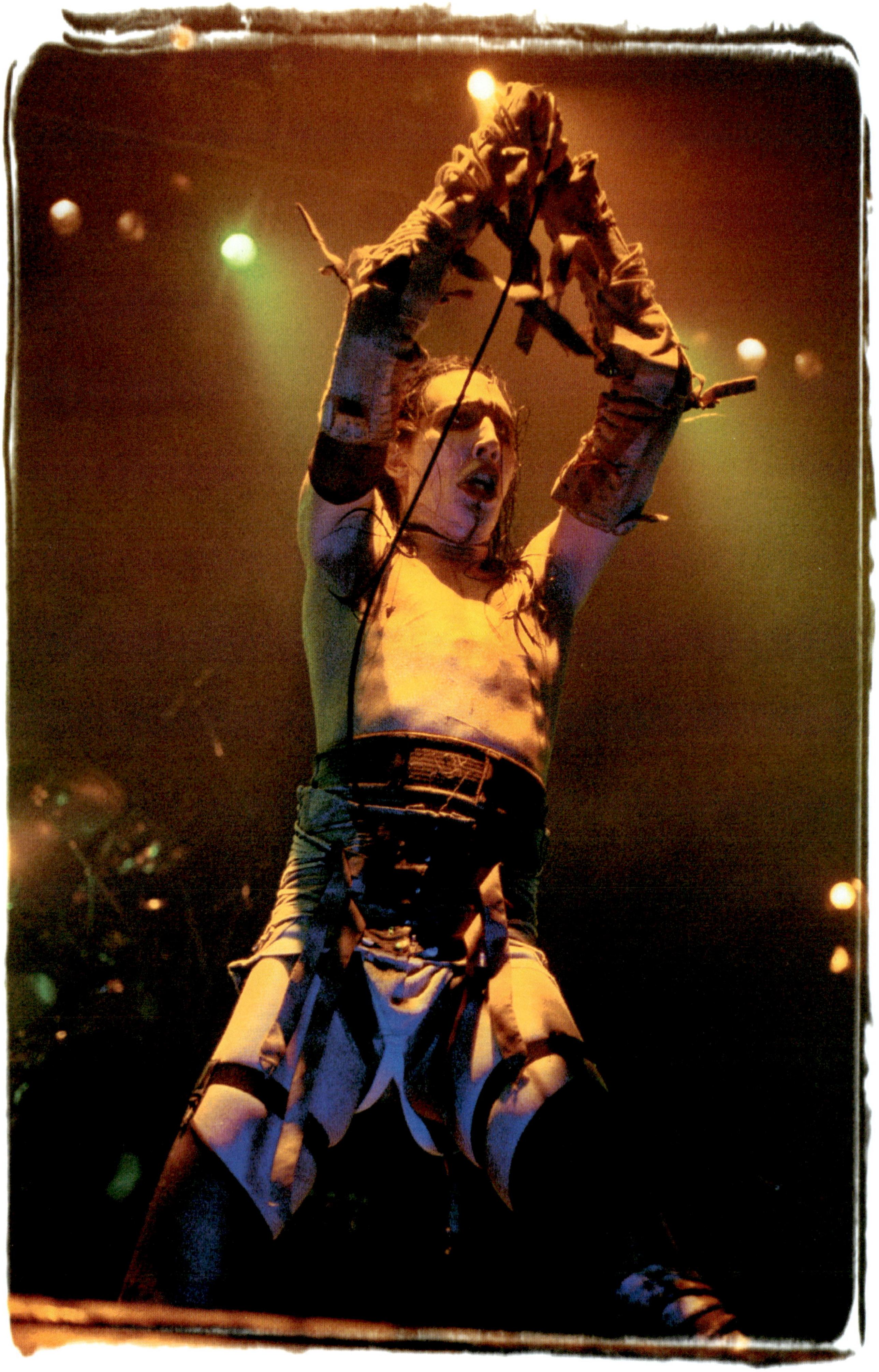

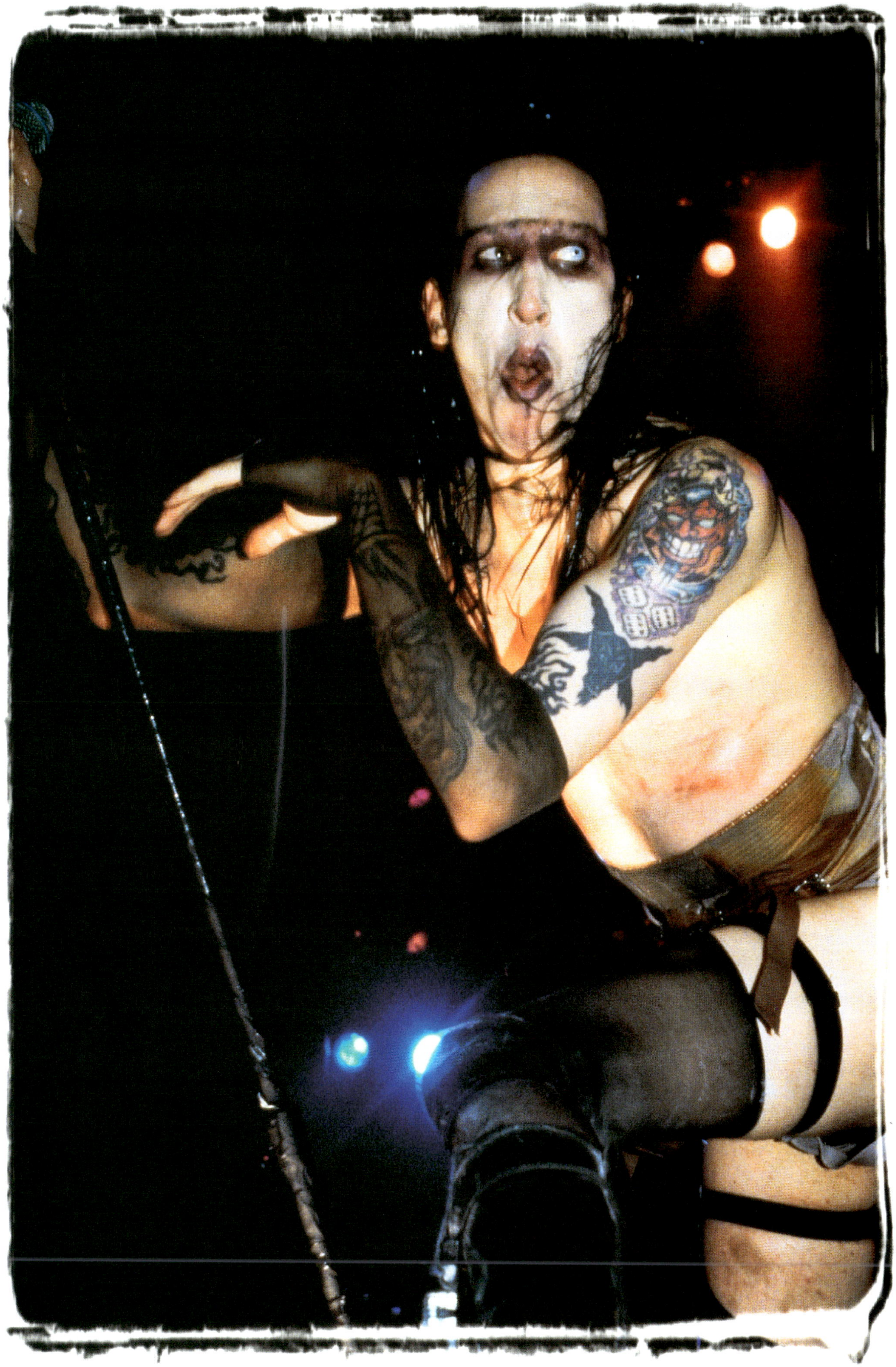

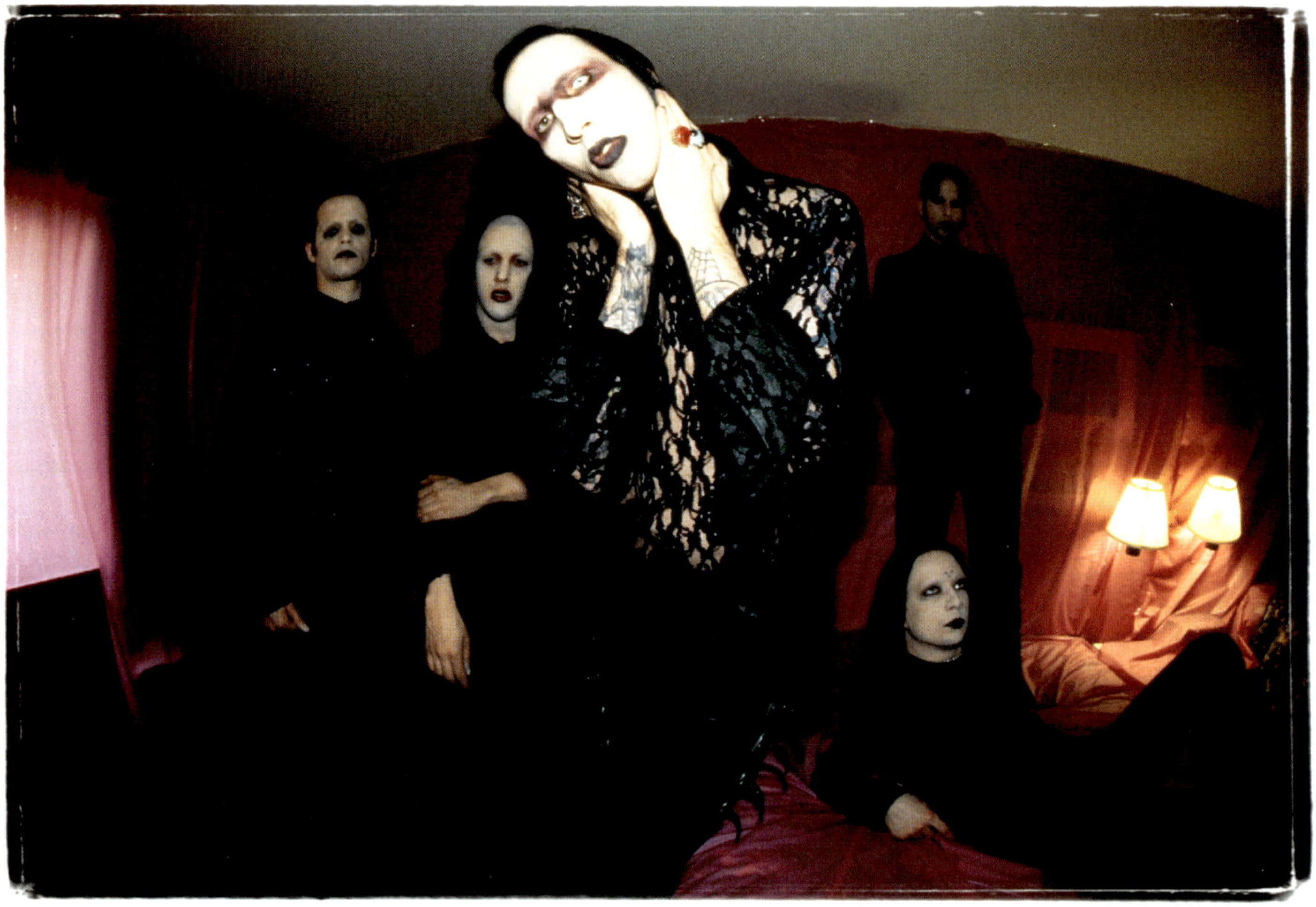

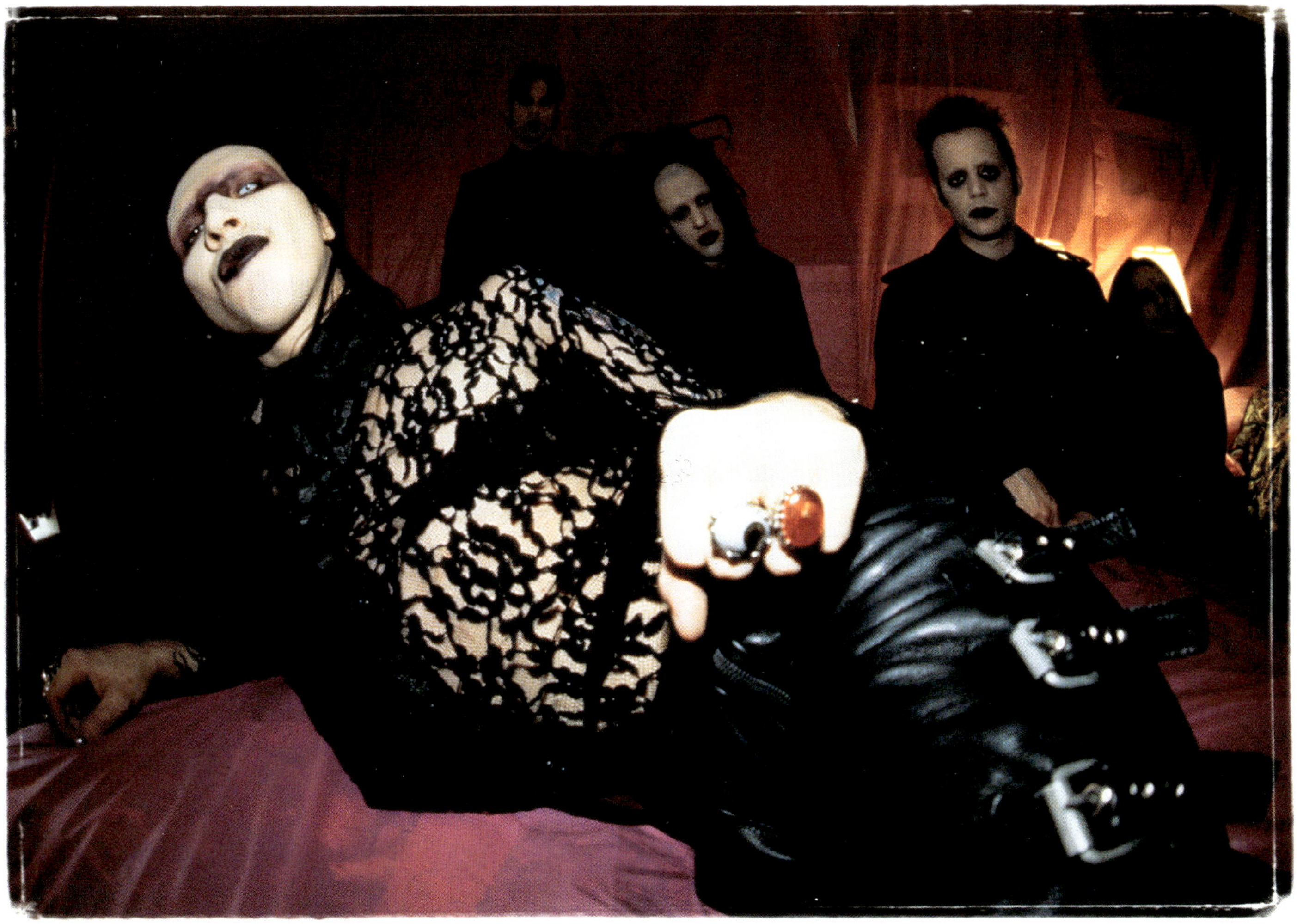

reported on May 3, 1997, that the concert was rescheduled "after city officials realized they could be violating the band's First Amendment rights." All with a little help from the American Civil Liberties Union, who stand behind Marilyn Manson's right to perform.

Ironically, the only trouble the "Dead to the World" tour has seen has been before the shows; the concerts themselves have gone, as the band's attorney Paul Cambria told *Billboard*, "without a hitch." Booking agent Artist and Audience encourages worry-wart venue heads to check their facts by getting reports from previous concert-holders. Perhaps the most publicized hub of protest was Biloxi, Mississippi, where cries to cancel the April 12 show were particularly noisy. Bill Holmes, the director of the Mississippi Coast Coliseum, was quoted in *The Sun Herald* on March 26 as saying, "I want to cancel the show. I've got people saying I'm in bed with Satan." Interestingly, after the concert Holmes told *Billboard* that they "had no problems whatsoever" and went on to add that "We did not have one fight—not one unruly deal." Which, to anyone who has ever attended a rock concert, is quite an unheard-of statistic. Holmes was also interviewed by *Rolling Stone* it its June 12, 1997, issue, wherein he noted, "We've done Alice Cooper, Judas Priest, Kiss. But this was the granddaddy—unbelievable."

Well, being railed against by notoriously excitable Bible Belters is one thing, but you'd expect bigger and better of the rock 'n' rollers in New York City, now wouldn't you? Incredibly, the latest trend in concert cancelation caught on at Giants Stadium—and even more incredibly, the venue wanted to strike Marilyn Manson from the OzzFest '97 bill on June 15. That the original king of controversy, a man famed for biting the head off of a live rat onstage in his hey day, should put together a concert featuring the likes of Pantera, Type O Negative, and a reunion of Black Sabbath and be told that "all of that is just fine, as long as you don't bring that horrible Manson fellow with you" is nothing short of insulting! Ozzy Osbourne's public statement about the unfolding situation was, "Nobody has the right to tell me who I can perform with. . . . This is not an issue of taste. It is an issue of civil liberty and freedom." Of course, Ozzy has dealt with the moral majority before, and takes it all with a sense of humor; as he told *Rolling Stone* in their May 22, 1997, "Random Notes Daily," "It makes my heart feel wonderful when I hear that these idiots are coming out of their fucking attic again. I have to laugh." On April 28 Marilyn Manson, along with concert promoter Delsener/Slater and Ardee Festivals N.J. Incorporated, filed a lawsuit against the New Jersey Sports and Exposition Authority. The Director of Giants Stadium, Bob Castronovo, was quoted in the May 3, 1997, issue of *Billboard* as stating that "we will offer [OzzFest] a contract with our parameters in them, one of which gives us the right to choose the groups [for the show]." On May 7 the courts sided with our heroes and ruled that the show would go on, and that the Authority was neither to attempt to stop Marilyn Manson from performing as part of the concert nor to obstruct ticket sales in any way. The final word on the OzzFest? *Billboard Bulletin* July 9, 1997, ran an article entitled "OzzFest is a Surprise Success Story," noting that "the nine shows with shock rock act Marilyn Manson were among the most successful, includ-

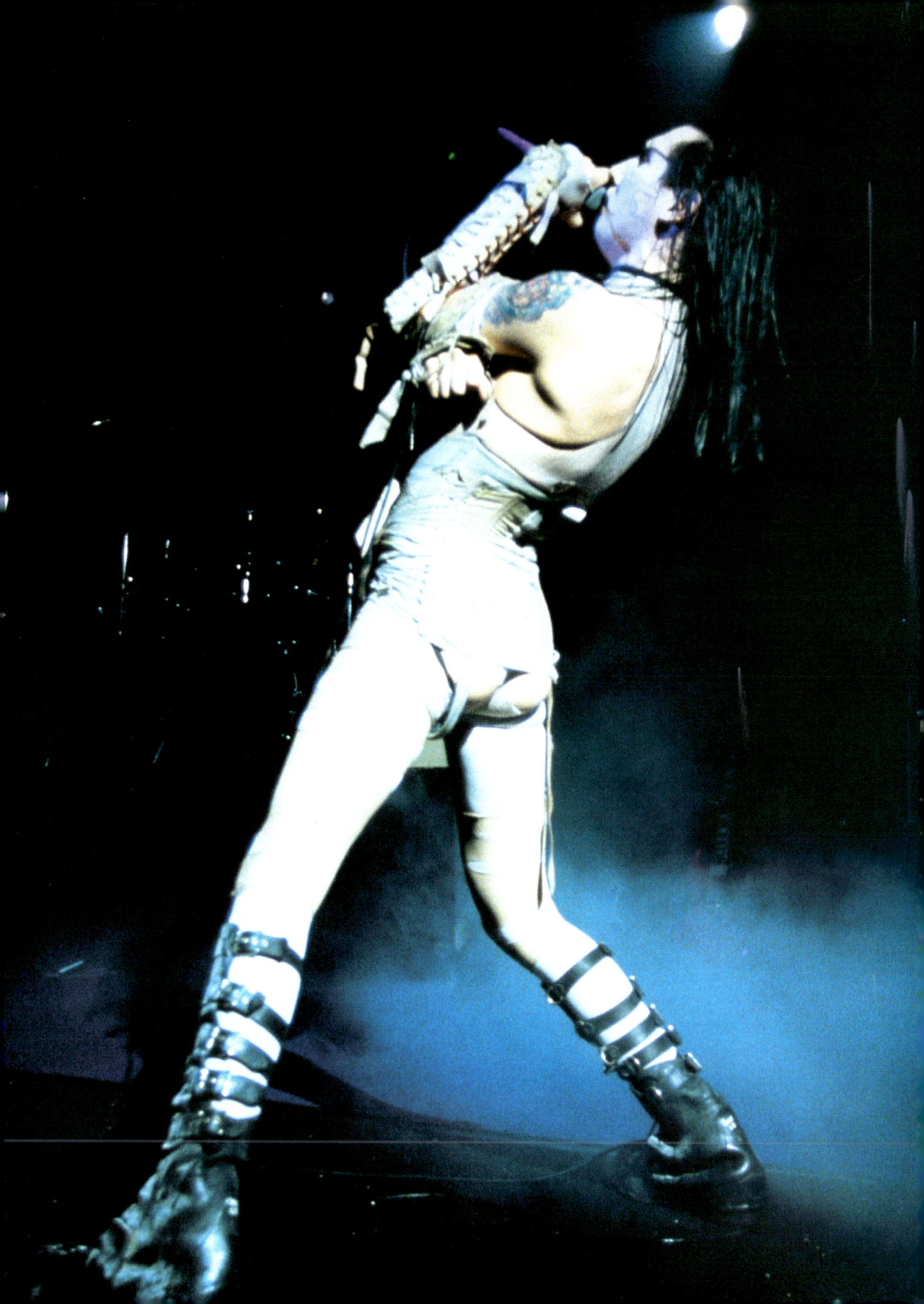

ing crowds of 32,500 in Minneapolis and 32,000 in Milwaukee." As Manson himself told *Metal Edge* magazine in its August 1997 issue, the OzzFest was "great, it's kind of like the old school coming together with the new school, because I know Ozzy's gone through a lot of the same things that I'm going through right now."

Well, there's nothing like a bit of outrage and protest mixed with rock 'n' roll to fire up the media. Not to be left out of a sensational story in the making, *Rolling Stone* featured a stamp across its June 12 cover reading "The Plot Against Marilyn Manson." The article itself, entitled "How the Christian Right is trying to run Marilyn Manson off the road" was a veritable *Sixty Minutes*–style research into the convoluted and truly incredible trail of anti-Manson propaganda. Conservative groups such as the American Family Association, the Christian Family Network, Empower America, and the Oklahomans for Children and Family were reported to be circulating so-called factual information on the band via the mail, fax, and most rampantly over the Internet, including "affidavits" detailing common occurrences at Manson gigs such as "animal sacrifices, sex with dogs, rapes, and heavy drug use," to name but a few.

The American Family Association's official web page boasted an entire section devoted to "Marilyn Manson Info" (info being an abbreviation for information, apparently in the broadest sense of the term), featuring "Media Reports & Eye-Witness Accounts of recent concerts," "Things Parents and Youth Ministers need to know about Marilyn Manson," and the "National Clearinghouse on Marilyn Manson Concerts for Family & Decency Advocates." Yet another unfounded anti-Manson claim was to be found in the A.F.A.'s June 20, 1997, on-line press release which noted that "the band's music has been tied to at least two teen suicides." The enthusiasm with which these reports were broadcast and distributed (to the police, churches, schools, state and local governments) and the eagerness with which they were taken as gospel truth was truly astounding.

The fervor stopped short, however, at the notion of verifying the accuracy of any of the disinformation.

The A.F.A.'s Manson-related activities and web site prompted the formation of The Portrait of An American Family Association and its own inspired website dedicated to spreading the down-and-dirty truth about Marilyn Manson, its music, concerts, and Mr. Manson's message. The Washington State Chapter of the P.O.A.A.F.A. states on its web page that "it is our goal to put an end to the outrageous rumors and slanders that have plagued this band since its release of the *Antichrist Superstar* CD. By doing this we hope to prevent the banning of further Marilyn Manson concerts so that others can choose for themselves if they desire to support or criticize this unique band." The logical, responsible, and well-researched P.O.A.A.F.A. web page urges Manson fans to respond to false accusations about the band by e-mailing, faxing, writing, and otherwise spreading the word to the likes of the A.F.A. and other church and government organizations, cautioning fans to "be polite but tell the truth," and offers an educational flyer for downloading. If a Manson fan encounters a protestor outside of a concert, he is encouraged by the P.O.A.A.F.A. to keep a stiff upper lip in the face of fanatical chanting and offer the flyer (entitled "Marilyn Manson Facts: What the religious right *doesn't* want you to know" and written by none other than angelynx–a.k.a. Paula O'Keefe–a high-profile, intelligent, and articulate fan and on-line contributor to many a Marilyn Manson web page) as a retort.

Marilyn Manson himself, who has never been known to give the proverbial rat's ass what people say about him, even began to get a little pissed off at the preposterous claims of the self-appointed guardians of America's pseudo-morals. He doesn't mind a bit of dissension—in fact he applauds it—but would prefer for it to be remotely reality-based. As he told *Rolling Stone* in its June 26, 1997, issue, "I don't have a problem with someone who opposes me or wants to try and stop a show because they think that Marilyn Manson contributes to the decay of Western civilization, or if someone doesn't want to buy an album

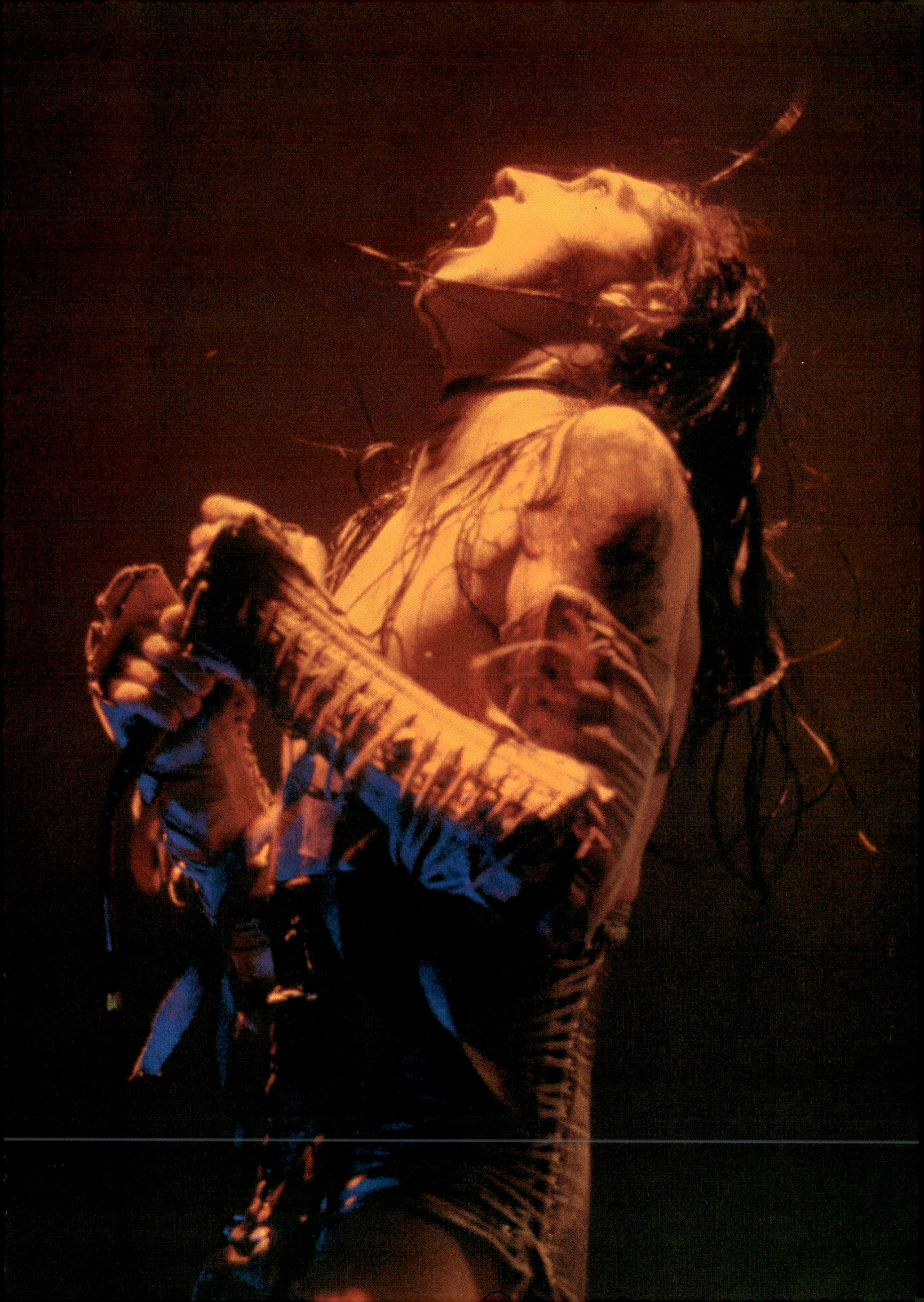

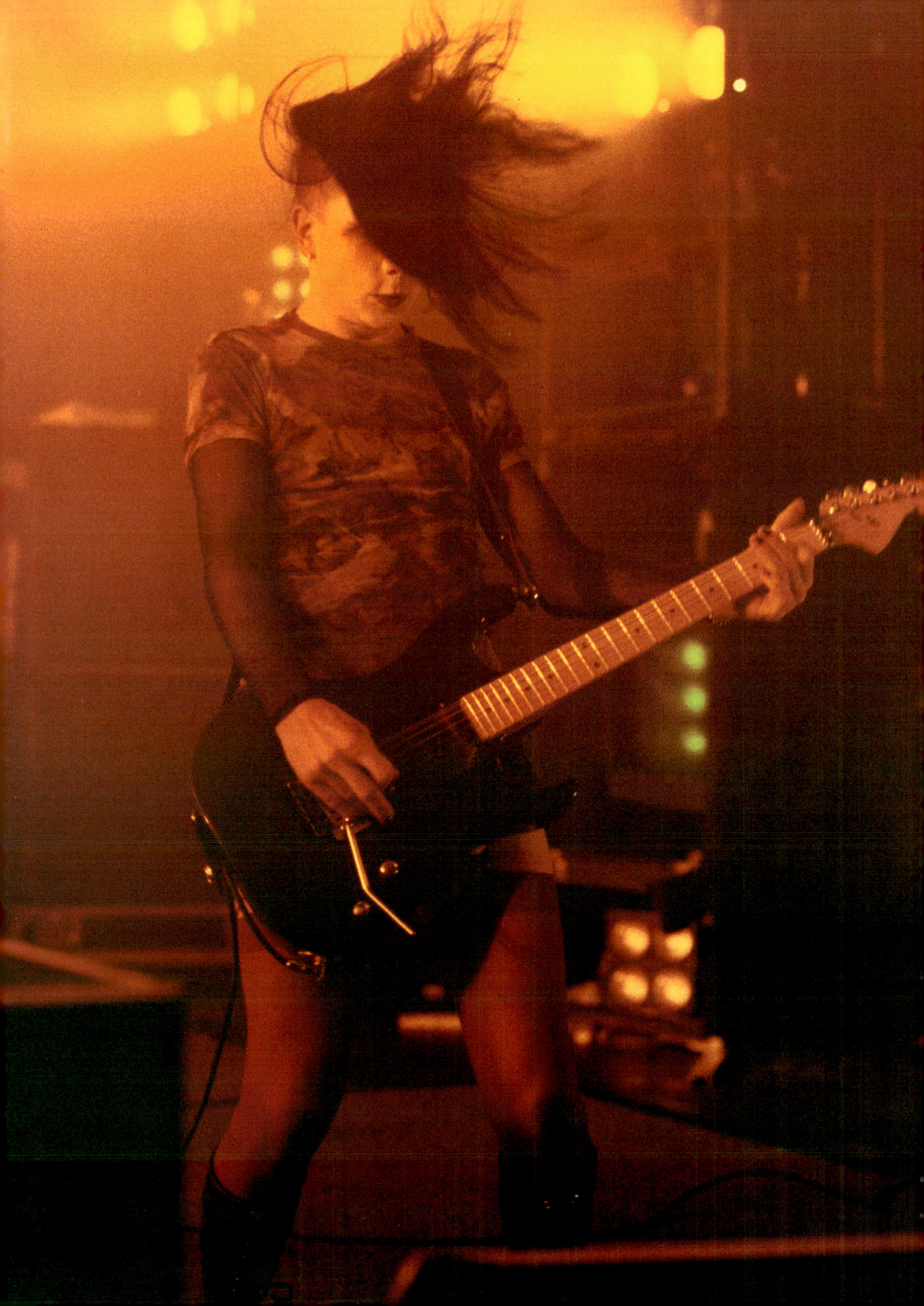

because they think it sucks. But these people didn't just disagree with my message. They completely *ignored* my message." In his first public retort to some of the Internet-posted "reports" of his gigs, he puts himself across as much more reasonably minded than his detractors. To claims that he kills puppies on stage he states, "I like dogs. I have a dog." To allegations that he has a squad of "private Santa Clauses" who distribute drugs to the audience, he scoffs, "That is ridiculous. If I had a giant bag of drugs, I would not be passing them out, especially for free. I would be backstage doing them." Of the various violent and sexual acts of which he has been accused, Manson has often queried how he is supposed to have performed such deeds - some of which are felonies - in front of thousands of people without being handcuffed and carted off to the Big House. Indeed, video-camera-wielding but inevitably disappointed members of many a police department have allegedly presided over Manson concerts in the hopes of catching an illegal act or two on tape to no avail.

To protest that his on-stage persona and behavior is outrageously indecent and offensive, Manson has an unperturbed commonsense rebuttal. "Some of it might be tasteless for some people, but then who told them to look?" he asked *Circus* magazine in June of 1997. "I don't know if it's tasteless or not, a lot of it is exciting to me. I do whatever I want, I'm discovering myself on and off stage." With an intuitive leap of reasoning, Manson has even managed to turn the tables on the likes of the A.F.A., stating in the August 1997 issue of *Metal Edge*, "It's ironic to me because these people have taken such an interest in pornography and filth and deviant behavior, that they've obtained the ability to dream up some very perverted fantasies, and I think if they're pointing the finger at me being sick, they should look at who's making up the stories." In fact, Manson actually mourns the loss of innocence; as he told *Metal Hammer* in July 1997, "In America, nothing excites anybody anymore. I'd have loved to have lived in a time when looking up a girl's skirt was exciting." On the other hand, he adds, "If it will make people happy to experiment sexually, then fine, that'll make me happy, because I like to hear of people doing more than sitting in front of the TV and doing the acceptable."

As for the band's documented views on religion, they are decidedly straightforward. "Going to confession and being 'clean' afterwards is not our idea of how it should work. It helps people to avoid responsibility," Twiggy Ramirez explained to *Circus* magazine in its May 20, 1997, issue. Manson admitted to *Guitar World* in December 1996, "I'm very much opposed to Christianity, but most of my values are something that Jesus might have preached" and told *SPIN* that the *Antichrist Superstar* album "will be America's God's punishment for the sins that they've created for themselves, and hopefully, I'll be remembered as the person who brought an end to Christianity." "Because we tell people that we are against organized religions doesn't mean we burn down churches or worship the devil. We have our own religion and some parts of it are even identical with some Christian beliefs," Twiggy told *Circus*. As Manson summed it up to *Metal Edge* in August 1997, "America has left a very dirty taste in my mouth when it comes to the idea of God."

At times, however, Mr. Manson seemed to take it all with a pinch of salt, keeping in mind that age-old showbiz adage that there's no such thing as bad publicity, reasoning that "if people really care about fighting off so-called 'problems' like Marilyn Manson, they would actually choose to ignore us. The more they bitch about us, the more attention they give us." "I thought we were in a different day and age where people were intelligent enough to understand art and music. Apparently that's not the case," he quipped to *Metal Edge* in August 1997. However, his core view on the situation is that it is a serious one indeed. As he told *Metal Edge* in its August 1997 issue, "It's just gotten to the point where I feel like I'm the only one fighting for rock music in general, because these people are just trying to take away my right—to take away everyone's right—to not only hear what they want but to say and do what they're entitled to under the First Amendment. It's become a full-on revolution for me." Well, isn't that just what he wanted? A revolution? And true to his prophetic word, that's just what he's got.

# ANGELWORMS

In keeping with the original Marilyn Manson ethic of celebrating the opposing extremes of life, just as many people adored Manson and his music as despised him. As Manson put it to *Alternative Press* in its February 6, 1997, issue, "I've always found that there are two kind of people in the world; people who like Marilyn Manson and people who are jealous." In fact, some factions of society found him extremely entertaining. Antichrist aside, he has most certainly become a superstar, and anyone who looks like that and gives a hell of an interview deserves a bit of attention.

Turning up here, there, and everywhere, Marilyn Manson and his cohorts soon found themselves in the public eye like never before. Awards were no longer confined to the microcosmic Slammies. The "Sweet Dreams" video found itself up against seasoned professionals like Metallica in the MTV Awards. In 1996 Marilyn Manson was inducted into Cleveland's Rock 'n' Roll Hall of Fame. *Hit Parader*'s 1997 Reader Survey saw Marilyn Manson voted "Favorite Band." Mr. Manson's photo began surfacing in publications of all description. He was snapped standing next to Billy Corgan, making even the Smashing Pumpkins frontman look like a suntanned picture of health. *SPIN*'s Special Twelfth Anniversary Issue "The SPIN 40" featured a suitably disturbed-looking Manson, complete with dead duck, as number 22, dubbing our hero "one scary monster, one super creep." Praise indeed.

Rumors began making their fast and furious way through the undergrowth: Manson to commit suicide on Halloween, Manson will be having a single breast implant, Manson spread blood on a baby while giving an autograph (he claims it was lipstick), Manson cut off his own testicles. Manson engaged in a sex act on stage with Nine Inch Nails guitarist Robin Finck while his parents were in the audience. And, of course, perhaps the most famed rumor of all . . . as Mr. Manson himself put it to *Metal Edge*, August 1997, "People said that I removed my two bottom ribs so that I could perform oral sex on myself. But that's untrue. The operation was far too expensive."

Manson, with date Twiggy Ramirez, turned up at Howard Stern's *Private Parts* February 28, 1997, premiere party at New York's Madison Square Garden. The Reverend Manson looked quite respectable—relatively speaking—in suit and tie, and was quoted as professing to tune in to the King of All Media's show "when I've been up all night doing drugs." The *Private Parts* soundtrack, boasting acts such as AC/DC and Porno for Pyros, has its requisite Marilyn Manson original in the song "The Suck for Your Solution." Party guests included Rob Zombie, Robin Quivers, Manson who was accompanied, according to *SPIN* magazine, by a blonde "nude masseuse," Conan O'Brien, Joey Buttafucco and his lawyer . . . the list goes on. Manson reportedly partied on until the wee hours with fellow rock stars Billy Corgan, Anthrax, Alice in Chains, and Perry Farrell. At the Thirty-ninth Annual Grammy Awards in April, Rob Zombie was interviewed before the show and was quoted in *Rolling Stone* as declaring, "Some of the guys in Nine Inch Nails and Marilyn Manson are back at the hotel. We're all gonna watch it there—that's how it'll be fun." Difficult as it may be to imagine Trent, Twiggy, and gang snuggled up in their jammies in front of the set eagerly awaiting some room-service beers to arrive, we have to take Mr. Zombie's word for it. Manson even made his big screen debut in who other than David Lynch's film *The Lost Highway*. His part? A porno star, of course. He and Twiggy appeared in the opening scene of the film, in which Manson is naked and dead. So, it seemed, the Reverend Manson was quite capable of hanging out with the beautiful people after all. Of course, infiltration is always a spy's first mission, and how better to meet new allies?

As press coverage rose to a fevered pitch in the States, the UK was forced to sit up and take a bit of notice of the Manson crew. For a nation of sharp-tongued and dry-wit-

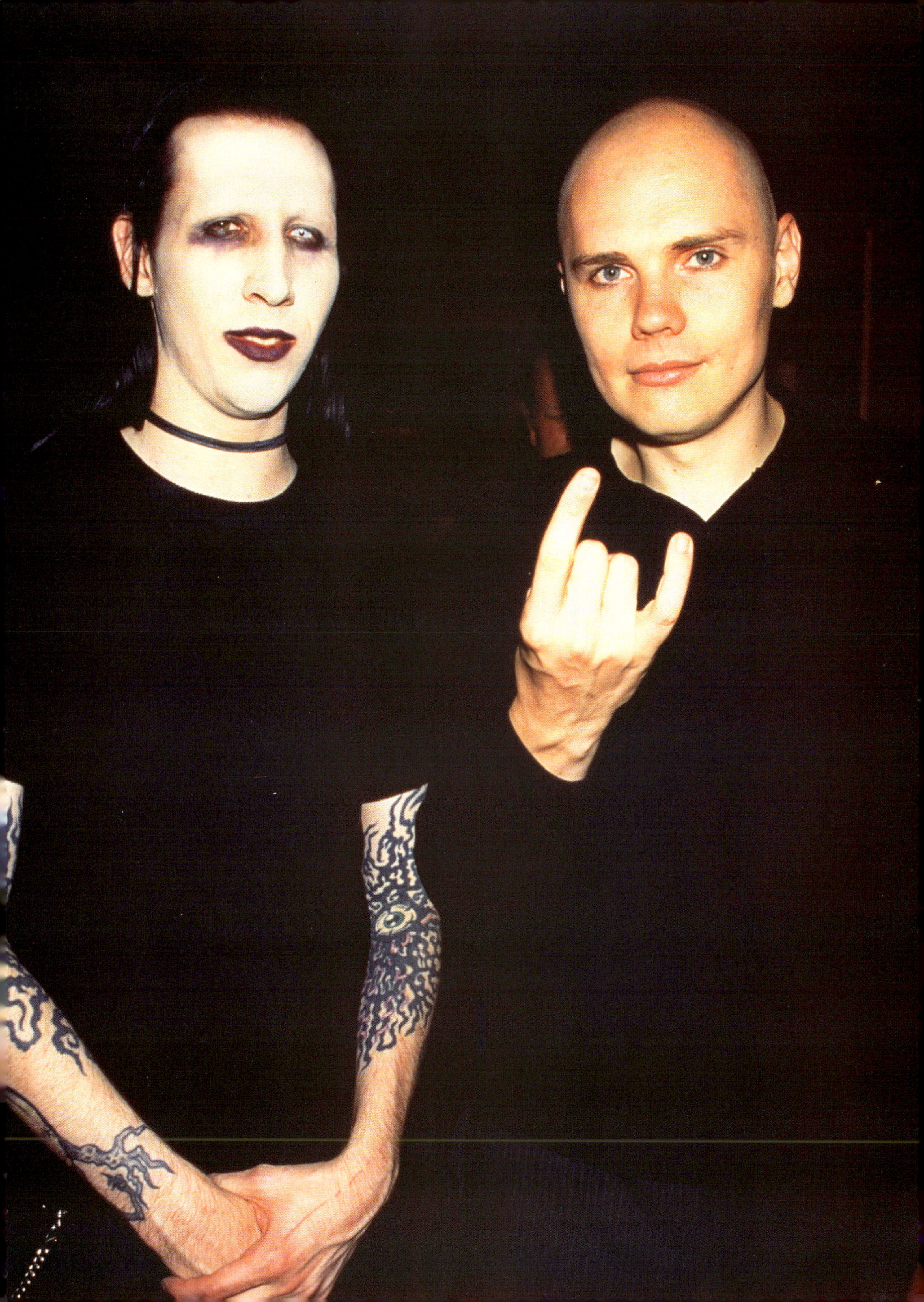

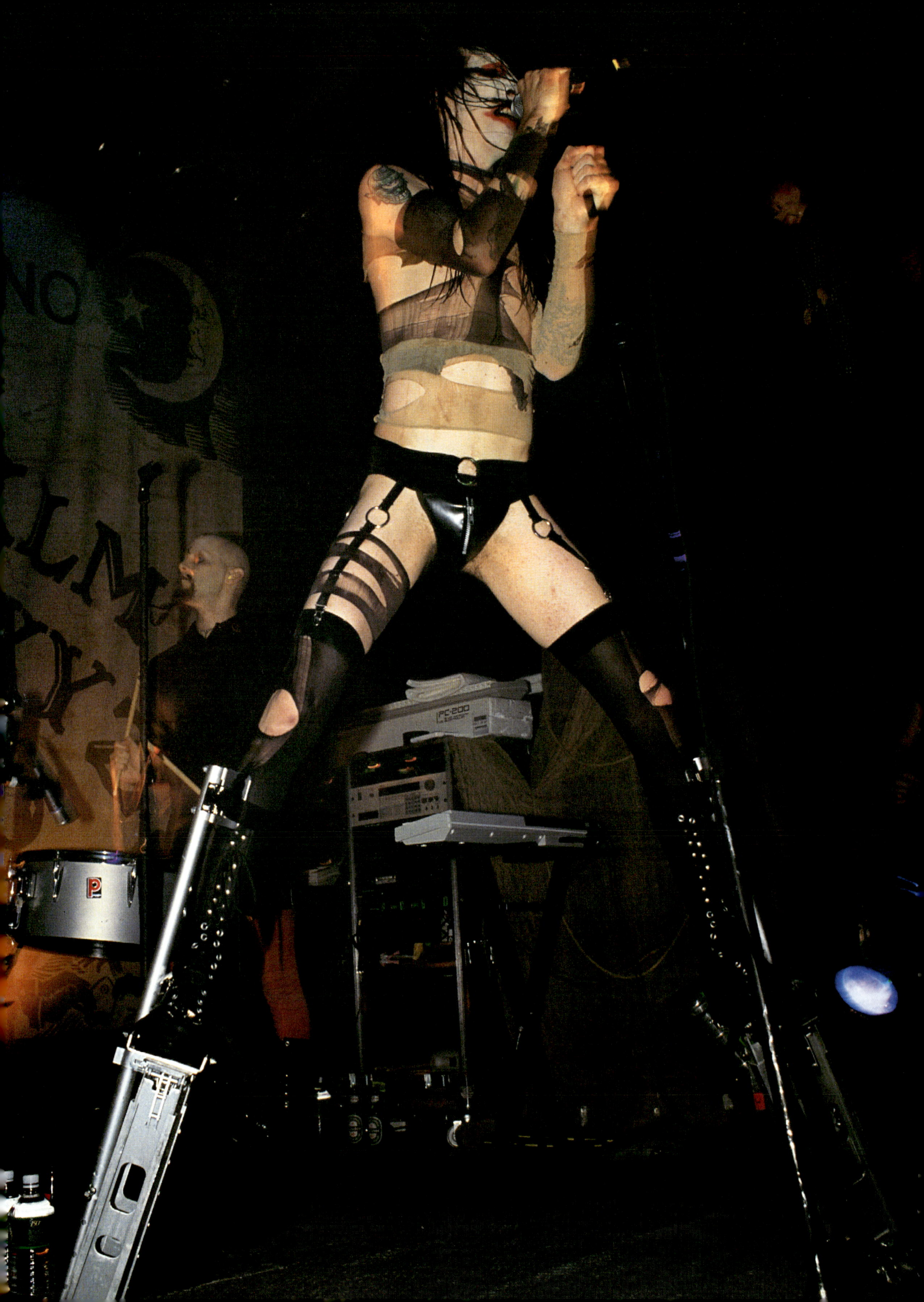
PC-200

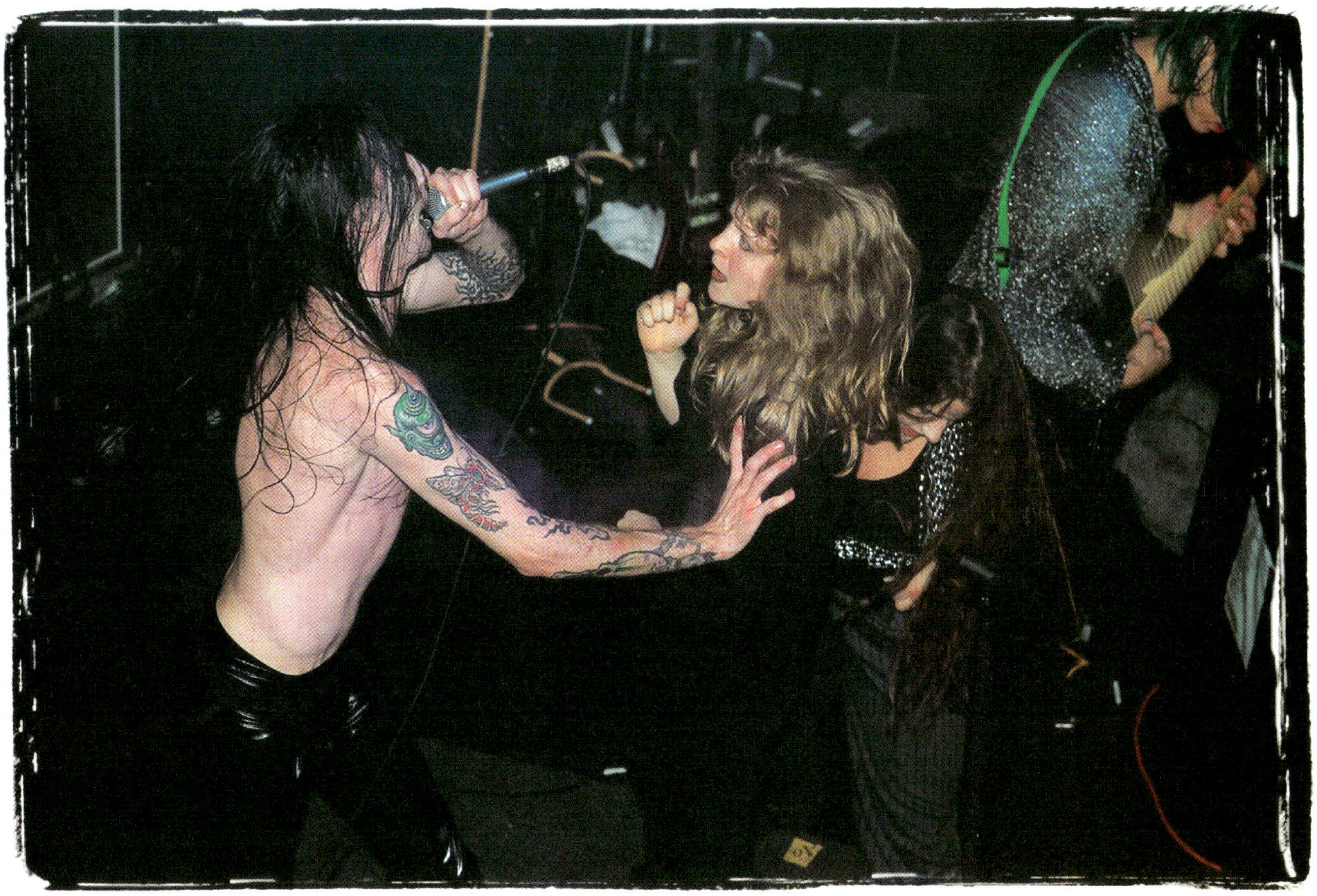

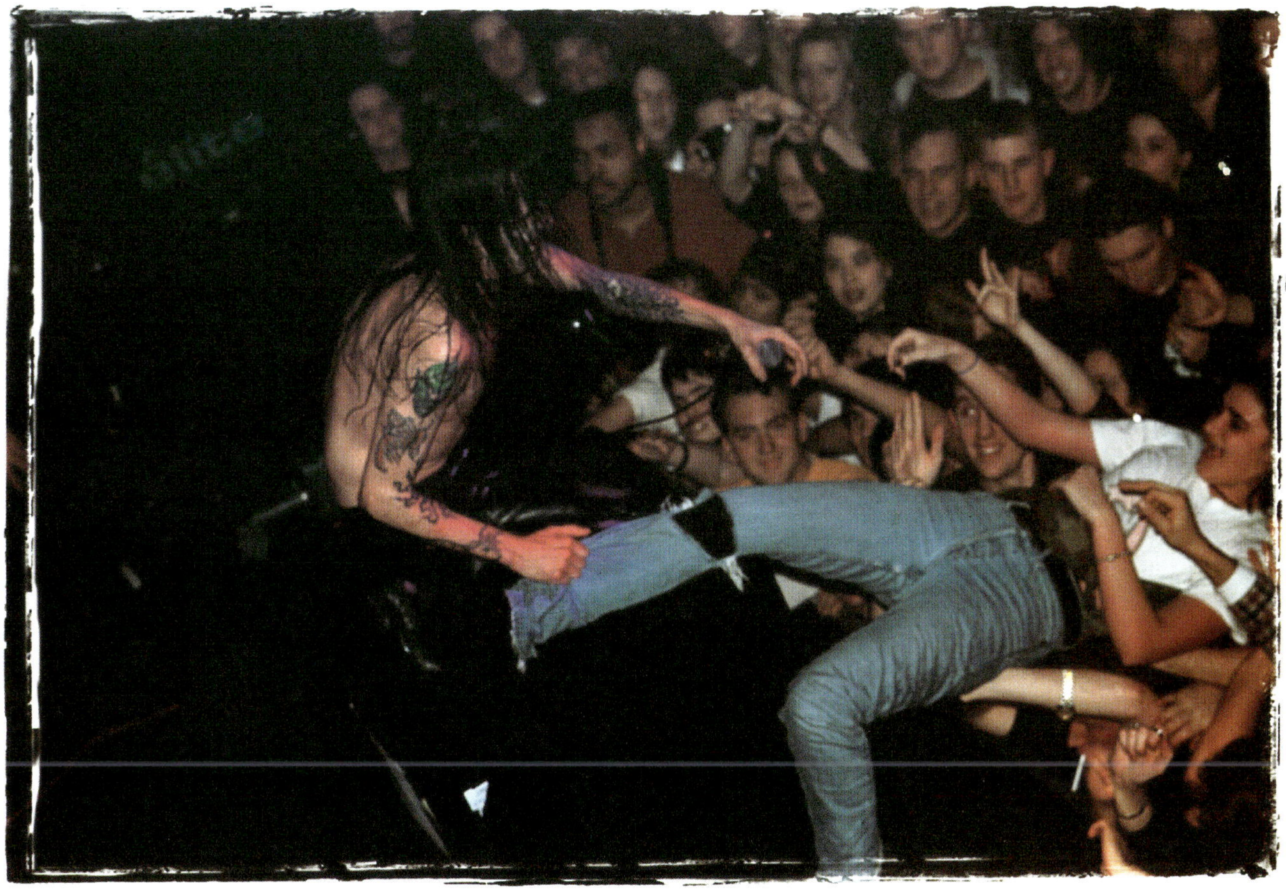

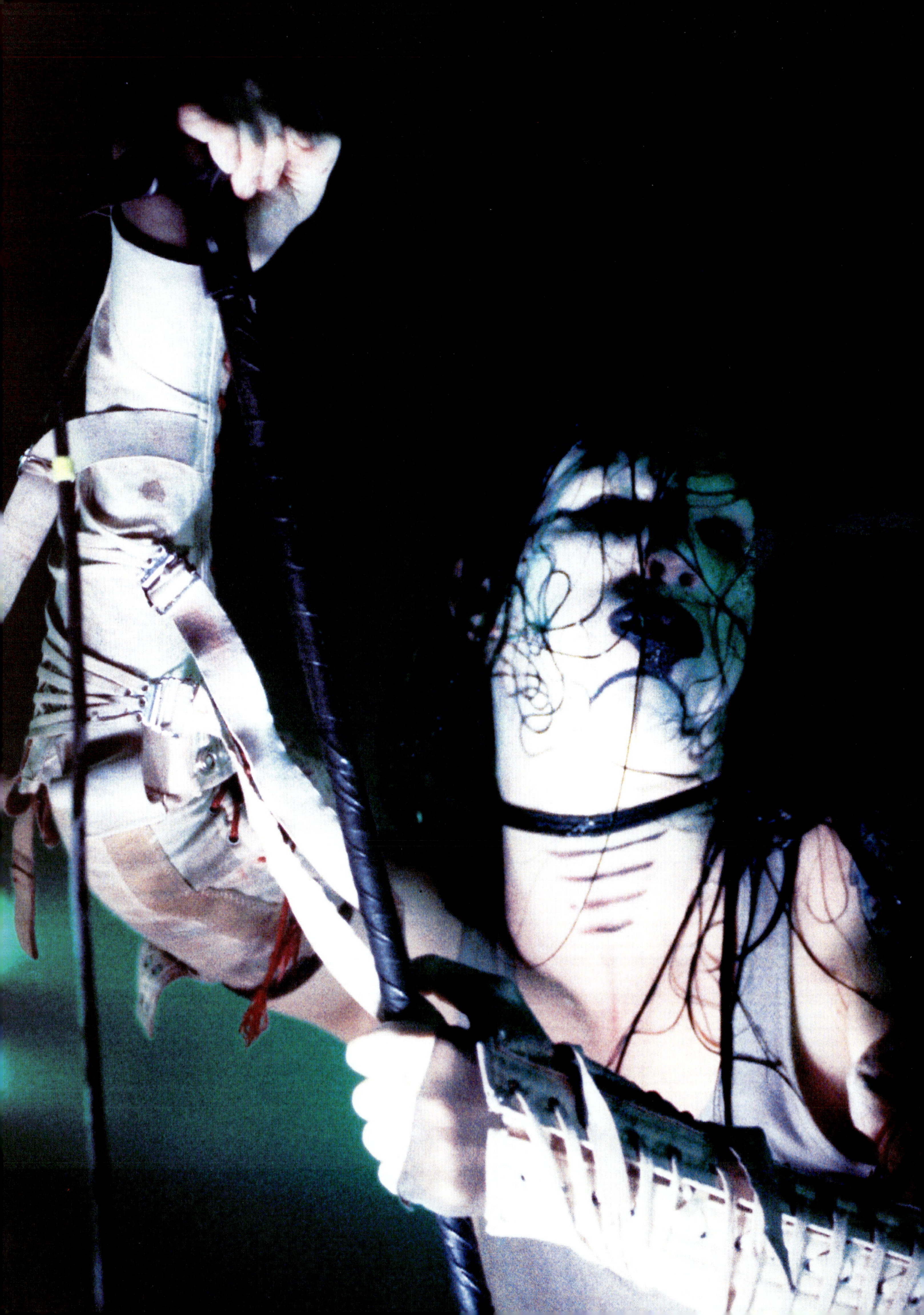

ted music critics for whom cynicism is a career requirement, the Reverend Manson got off fairly lightly. *Q*, the self-professed "World's Greatest Music Magazine" featured a large photo of the band members posing in all their glory around a hospital stretcher with Manson, scarred and lacerated chest suitably bared, in the foreground seated in a wheelchair. The photo's caption read, "No way is their image contrived." A smaller live shot of Mr. Manson live onstage in his usual garter-belt and medical-brace regalia is captioned "He's got a girlfriend, you know." The article alternately refers to our hero as "not unlike a rack-stretched Iggy Pop in Alice Cooper garb" or a "pansticked taboo-smasher."

In fact, the European music scene seems to find Manson and Company quite palatable. Either that, or they haven't taken him seriously enough yet to realize what they have on their hands. At the Dynamo Festival in Eindhoven, Holland on May 18, the band performed with the like-minded likes of Type O Negative, Entombed, Cradle of Filth, Fear Factory, Helmet, and Korn. The official Dynamo Festival T-shirts rather unfortunately listed "Marilyn Monroe" as one of its participants. The UK heavy metal magazine *Metal Hammer*'s review of the gig noted that Mr. Manson "attacked" Zim Zum "in a fit of murderous intent" and that after the lead singer incited a mud fight "a great slop of shit smacked him straight in the mush." Even this sympathetic publication felt obliged to poke a little fun. The article header in the magazine's July 1997 issue read, "Ever seen your grandfather in French underwear, barking like a dog? Mr. Manson has. Some people have all the fun, eh, readers?"

The big question to most overseas media seems to be, "What is all the fuss about?" *Q* bemusedly reports that "America's neo-right have responded to this oddly childlike entertainment by taking the singer very seriously indeed." And *Metal Hammer* queries, "But what is it about Marilyn Manson that so many people in America have found so objectionable? To British eyes, the motley Manson entourage can easily be contained as a nightmare Jane's Addiction on an Alice Cooper trip. Bizarre certainly, but dangerous? Hardly." Well, that remains to be seen.

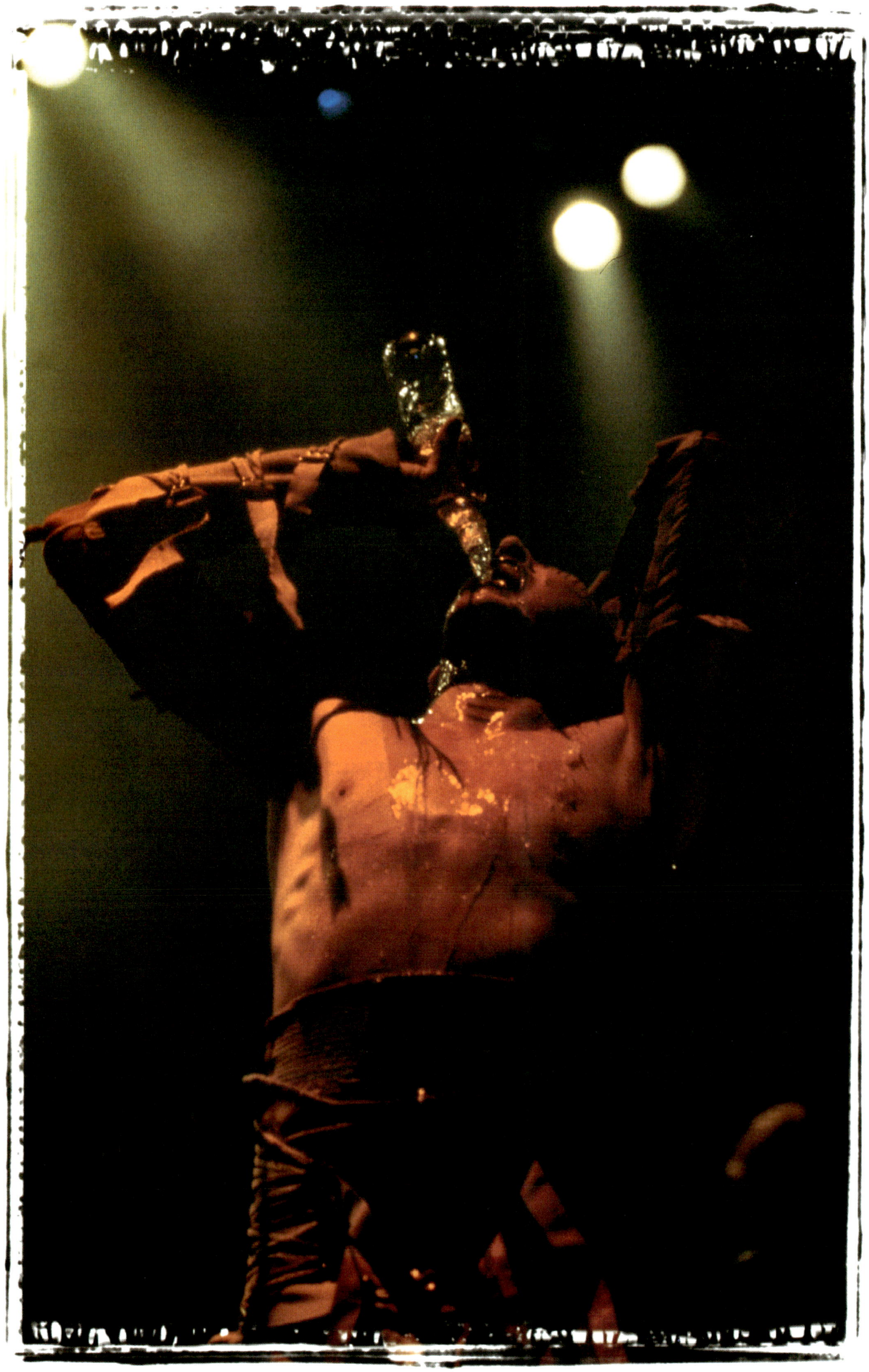

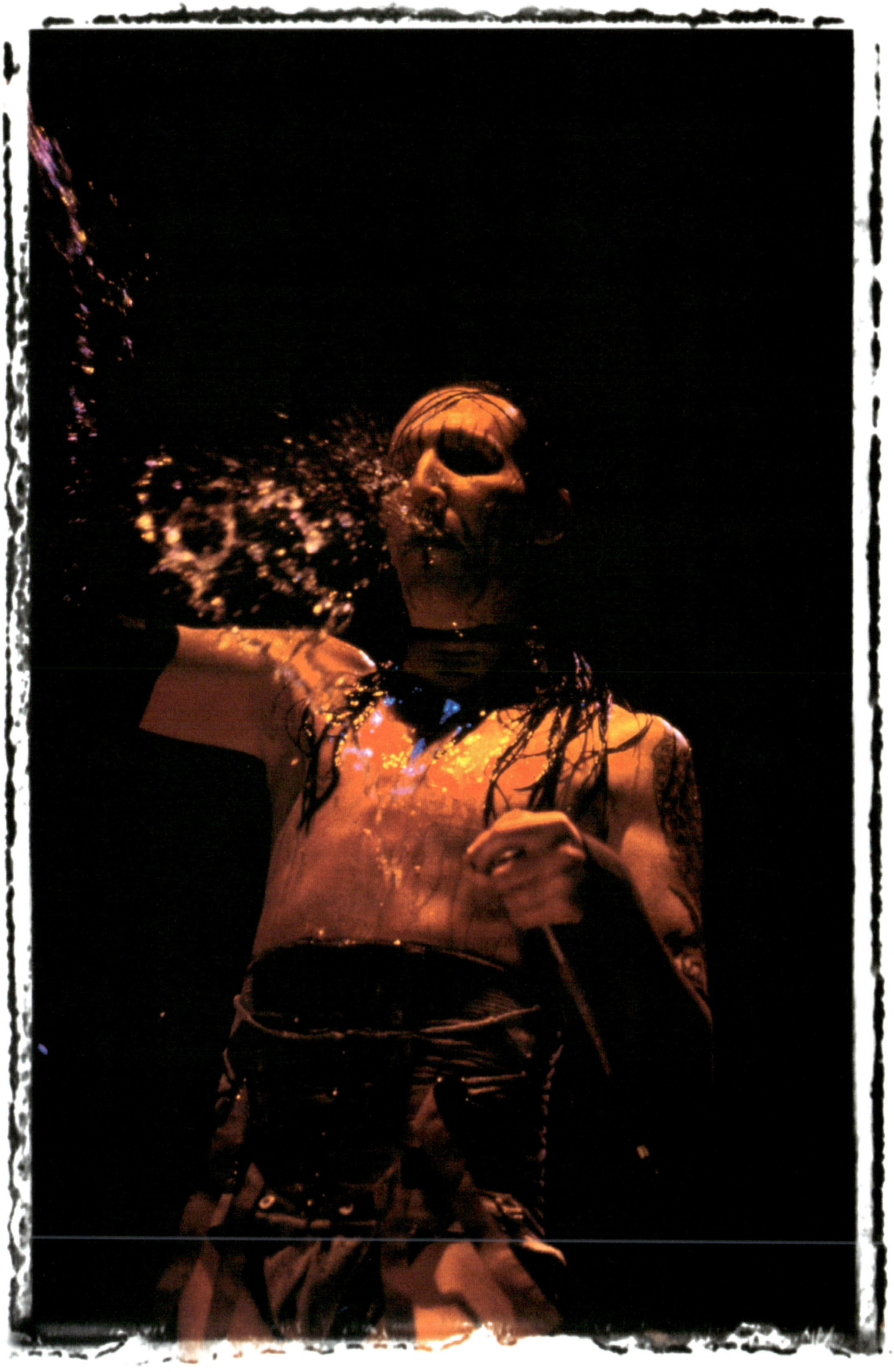

# TRICK or TREAT

Whether you find the Marilyn Manson troupe a curiosity or a danger, it is difficult to ignore them. Their videos are works of art that certainly provide an insight. The "Man That You Fear" video, directed by Wiz, was drastically different from the Manson MTV thought they had pegged. It is set somewhere in the middle of nowhere in what appears to be an American desert; trailer homes, buses, pregnant angels wearing halos, graveyards with bare crosses in place of tombstones all play a part. It is a definite departure from the frenetic, spastic, and oftentimes repulsive "Tourniquet" visuals, in fact, the slow pace of this almost sparse video is more dreamlike than nightmarish. The video begins with Manson being groomed—feet washed, hair combed, lipstick lovingly applied within the lines, corset tightly bound—by a woman who seems to be his lover. She leads him outside to join the band members and a dozen or so other "townspeople" including a little girl (daughter?) who holds Manson's hand as they all march through the desert in a parade of sorts. An American flag is part of the proceedings and Twiggy is ensconced in a tuba while Zim Zum carries a set of cymbals and Ginger Fish pounds on a bass drum. Manson, in a bizarre collar sprouting what looks to be long black horsehair, collapses half-way along, rising again only to be surrounded by the others (including his lover, who is now with child) who pick up stones from the dusty ground as they slowly circle him while he, seemingly submitting to his fate, tears at his shirt and looks up at the sky. These are not images that are easily shaken from the mind.

Even photographs of the band are difficult to glance over. Manson himself is consistently disconcerting at best. Whether in white (ruffled women's knickers and undershirt accessorized with lace-up surgical trusses on his arms) or in black (gas mask, layers of ripped stockings, and miscellaneous garter belts), he is at once repellent and fascinating. Madonna Wayne Gacy's bald head and Fu-Manchu beard still manage to look shockingly ugly even in a day and age when shaved skulls and goatees are *de rigueur* for any self-respecting young hipster roving the urban streets. Zim Zum has adopted the garter and stocking motif while remaining fairly conventional in crushed velvet tops and shorts, and flaunts an immaculately cut and shiningly groomed coif straight out of a Vidal Sassoon advertisement. It is difficult to decide if he looks glamorous or lifeless, or, even worse, both. Ginger Fish has taken to wearing formidable military gear. Twiggy Ramirez has given new meaning to the phrase "the walking dead." In fact, his look is that of a corpse—rudely unearthed after a long sleep during which its hair carried on growing—that spent more than a little time hanging out in a swamp before braving the modern world inappropriately garbed in a woman's housecoat from the 1950s.

Marilyn Manson without a doubt is quite a sight, and their music something tantalizing and terrifying. Certainly a bit of a shaking-up was overdue for the nineties music scene. As Manson told *Alternative Press* in its February 6, 1997, issue, "Apparently I'm gonna be the one that has to break my back to make rock music exciting again, because not too many other people are making the effort." After a cursory glance at the soundtrack-packed *Billboard* charts of the last few years, any vaguely informed music fan would have to agree that, well, he's got a point. But to experience the band in their element at a live performance is to really enter into their distorted world, and to realize that this is not just an act. For those who have assumed that the wormlike gyrations and fast-forward twitching in Marilyn Manson music videos are the product of a director's skill and high-tech camera manipulations, check out a live gig to see that, vilely enough, it's all for real.

Whether or not the Oompa Loompa theme song from *Charlie and the Chocolate Factory* is played at Manson concerts to herald the imminent on-stage appearance of the man himself, the persona of "Antichrist Superstar" on stage is something to behold. A new ingredient—just a pinch of arsenal—to the show is the Hitleresque skit performed during the title track. Imagine a pulpit, and the Reverend Manson, looking perhaps more twisted and ter-

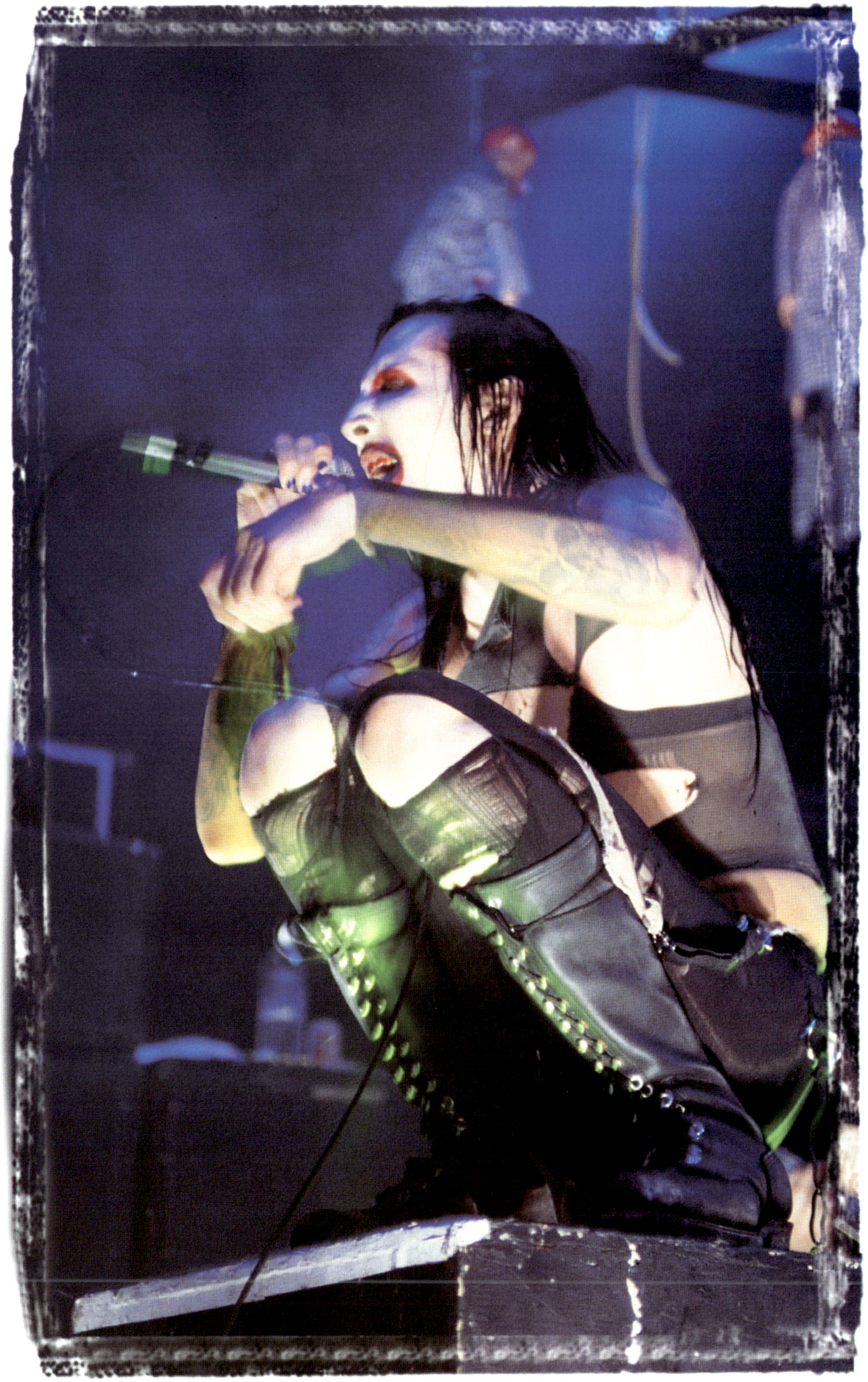

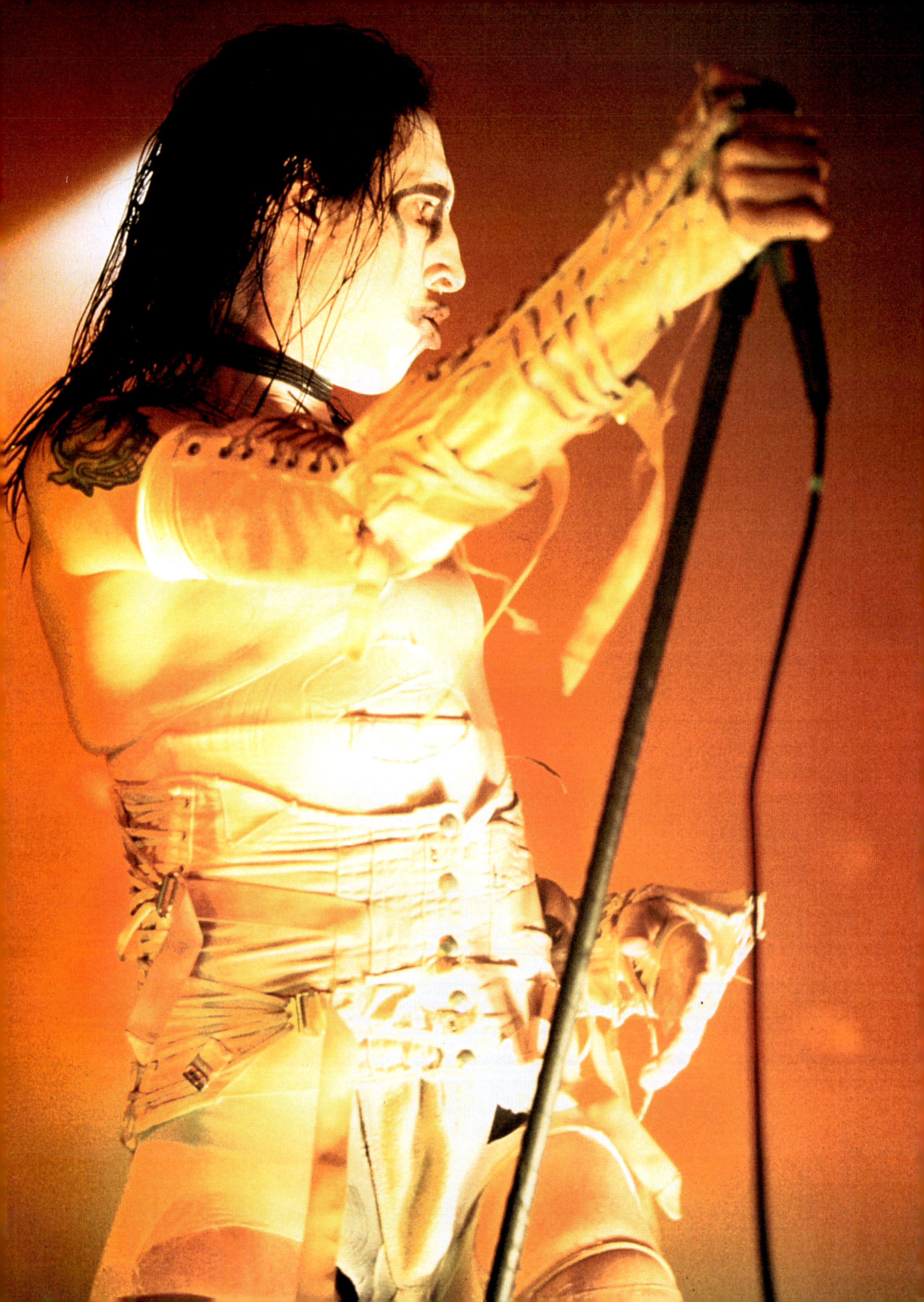

rifying than ever before in a polyester suit, masquerading as a full-on evangelist with a wife named Tammy Faye. Or is he a dictator conquering the audience from behind a podium bearing the album's signature electric-warning symbol (oft-accused of looking a tad too much like a swastika)? Either way, the effect is complete as the sold-out, sweaty crowd of disciples all dressed like hell raise their nasty little fists in the air to the chant, "Repent, that's what I'm talking about / Whose mistake am I anyway?" The object of all this is, no doubt, lost on many—particularly anti-Mansonites—and, as *Rolling Stone*'s "Random News Daily" reported on November 2, 1996, "Manson's point to show the audience how easily he can manipulate them is clearly made, and anyone that confuses this parody for fact is precisely whom Manson is trying to teach."

Nowadays, antics run the gamut, from spitting contests with front-row fans to Manson wiping his backside with an American flag. The classic Bible-shredding is still going strong—old habits die hard—and the stage set features an adult-size mobile of hanging male dolls. The audience is yet another facet of the experience. *Rolling Stone*'s "Random Notes Daily," in its review of the January 25 Santa Monica, California, show, cited "two girls in fluffy white sheep outfits, a large man in a wedding dress wearing a black yarmulke, a kid decked out in a priest's collar, a Goth couple with hair spiked a foot off their foreheads," and "a guy in a dress on stilts" as but a few members of the crowd. As Twiggy told *Circus* magazine in its July 15, 1996, issue, "I think we're the groupies. . . . I think we're in the audience and the crowd is on the stage. The fans are the ones who are the rock stars."

It has certainly been a bizarre trip down an unconventional, winding, spooky trail. But after all, the man who told *Rolling Stone* in its January 23, 1997, issue, "I feel like I've dreamed half of my life that hasn't happened yet. . . . I have déjà vus more than I have regular experiences" must have foreseen all the trouble. He certainly seems to be enjoying it. Whether he can see light at the end of Willie Wonka's tunnel remains to be seen, but the uprising he called for seems to be underway. As the Reverend Manson told *Alternative Press* in its February 6, 1997, issue, "I feel like the end of the world that I speak about is on a mental level; I see the apocalypse being the old-world mentality of Christianity dying off and something new being born—new individuality." Antichrist, superstar, both, or neither, he told *Metal Edge* in August 1997, "I think I'm really the voice that is speaking for everyone, and I think that everyone who is a fan or a friend is really a part of everything that I do, so it's one big machine. I think people will be surprised what a big machine can accomplish when it puts its mind to it." If recent events are any indication, we may be in for a very big surprise indeed.

# CHRONOLOGY

## 1989

Marilyn Manson and the Spooky Kids is formed by Marilyn Manson (vocals) and Daisy Berkowitz (guitar) in Ft. Lauderdale, Florida.

Official line-up is cemented with the addition of Madonna Wayne Gacy (keyboard) and Gidget Gein (bass).

Early gigs at Squeeze in Ft. Lauderdale.

## 1990-91

Sarah Lee Lucas joins the band, replacing the drum machine and becoming the first human drummer in the Spooky Kids line-up.

The first Marilyn Manson flyer is published, entitled "Marilyn Manson & the Spooky Kids: The Family Trip to Mortville."

## 1992

**JULY**
Marilyn Manson and the Spooky Kids win two Slammy Awards for Band of the Year and Best Hard Alternative Band.

**AUGUST**
The band shortens its name to Marilyn Manson.

## 1993

**MAY**
Marilyn Manson signs to Trent Reznor's Nothing Records, a division of Interscope Records.

**JULY**
Marilyn Manson win two Slammy Awards for Band of the Year and Song of the Year ("Dope Hat"). The self-produced *Family Jams* cassette is also nominated for Best Local Release.

**DECEMBER**
Twiggy Ramirez officially joins Marilyn Manson as bass player, replacing Gidget Gein.

## 1994

**JUNE**
The "Get Your Gunn" single is released.

**JULY 12**
*Portrait of an American Family* is released.

**JULY**
Marilyn Manson win Band of the Year Slammy Award, and Mr. Manson wins Best Vocalist Slammy Award.

"The Marilyn Manson Family Reality Transmission M1 (Fall 1994)" is published.

**AUGUST – DECEMBER**
Marilyn Manson is the support band for Nine Inch Nails' "Self Destruct" tour.

**OCTOBER**
Mr. Manson meets with Anton LaVey, the head of the Church of Satan, and is ordained Reverend Manson.

**October 18**
Delta Center, Salt Lake City, Utah gig famed for bible-shredding incident.

**December 27**
Club 5, Jacksonville, Florida gig at which Manson is arrested for "violation of the Adult Entertainment Code" and is jailed for one night.

## 1995

**JANUARY – MARCH**
Marilyn Manson tour in support of *Portrait of an American Family*.

**January 13**
Dallas, Texas gig at which a live chicken got loose on stage and caused consternation on the part of the United Poultry Concerns amongst other animal right's groups who claimed the chicken was "dismembered" by the audience.

**FEBRUARY**
Manson, Twiggy Ramirez, and Madonna Wayne-Gacy appear on the Phil Donahue Show as participants in a panel discussion on moshing.

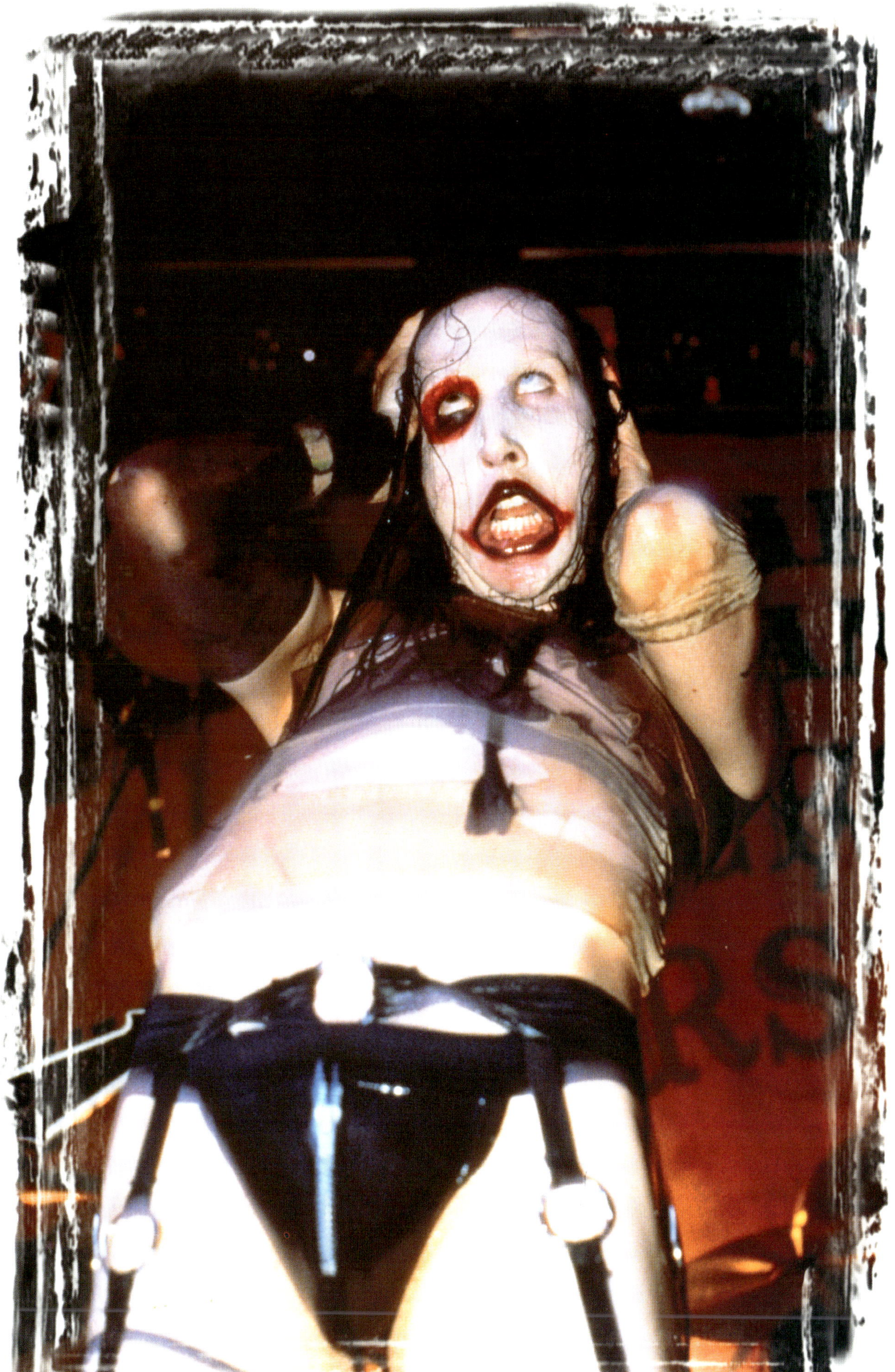

# CHRONOLOGY con't

## 1995 continued

**MARCH**
Sarah Lee Lucas leaves the band after he and his drum-set are set on fire during a gig.

Ginger Fish joins Marilyn Manson as drummer.

**MARCH – JUNE**
Marilyn Manson is the support band for Danzig's tour.

**June 22**
Marilyn Manson performs "Lunchbox" and "Dope Hat" on the Jon Stewart Show; Manson sets the stage alight.

Marilyn Manson win two Slammy Awards—Best National Release for *Portrait of an American Family* and Best Single for "Lunchbox."

**SEPTEMBER – DECEMBER**
Marilyn Manson tours.

**October 24**
The *Smells Like Children* EP is released.

## 1996

**JANUARY – FEBRUARY**
Marilyn Manson tours in support of *Smells Like Children*.

**MAY**
Daisy Berkowitz announces that he is leaving Marilyn Manson.

Zim Zum joins Marilyn Manson as guitarist.

Marilyn Manson are nominated for an MTV Video Music Award for Best Hard Rock Video for "Sweet Dreams (Are Made of This)."

**September 7**
Irving Plaza, New York City "Nothing Night" concert at which Marilyn Manson, Nine Inch Nails, and Meat Beat Manifesto perform; Ginger Fish is knocked unconscious during the show and is taken away in an ambulance.

**October 3**
Marilyn Manson's "Dead to the World" tour begins.

**October 8**
*Antichrist Superstar* is released, debuting at Number 3 on the Billboard charts.

**October 31**
Asbury Park, New Jersey gig at which it is rumored Manson will commit suicide and which is delayed due to a bomb threat.

Marilyn Manson is inducted into the Rock 'n' Roll Hall of Fame.

## 1997

Marilyn Manson appears in David Lynch's film, *The Lost Highway*.

**January 23**
Marilyn Manson graces the cover of *Rolling Stone* magazine. In the accompanying article, Manson is quoted as saying, "I was never afraid of what was under the bed. I wanted it. I wanted it more than anything. And I never got it. I just became it."

**March 22**
Honolulu, Hawaii gig at which Manson cuts an artery and is taken to the hospital by ambulance for stitches.

**April 20**
University of South Carolina gig is canceled; Marilyn Manson is allegedly paid $40,000 not to perform.

**May 10**
Richmond, Virginia gig takes place after being canceled and then re-scheduled.

**June 15**
Giants Stadium, New Jersey OzzFest gig is held; Marilyn Manson performs despite attempts by the venue to strike the band from the bill.

*All dates are approximate

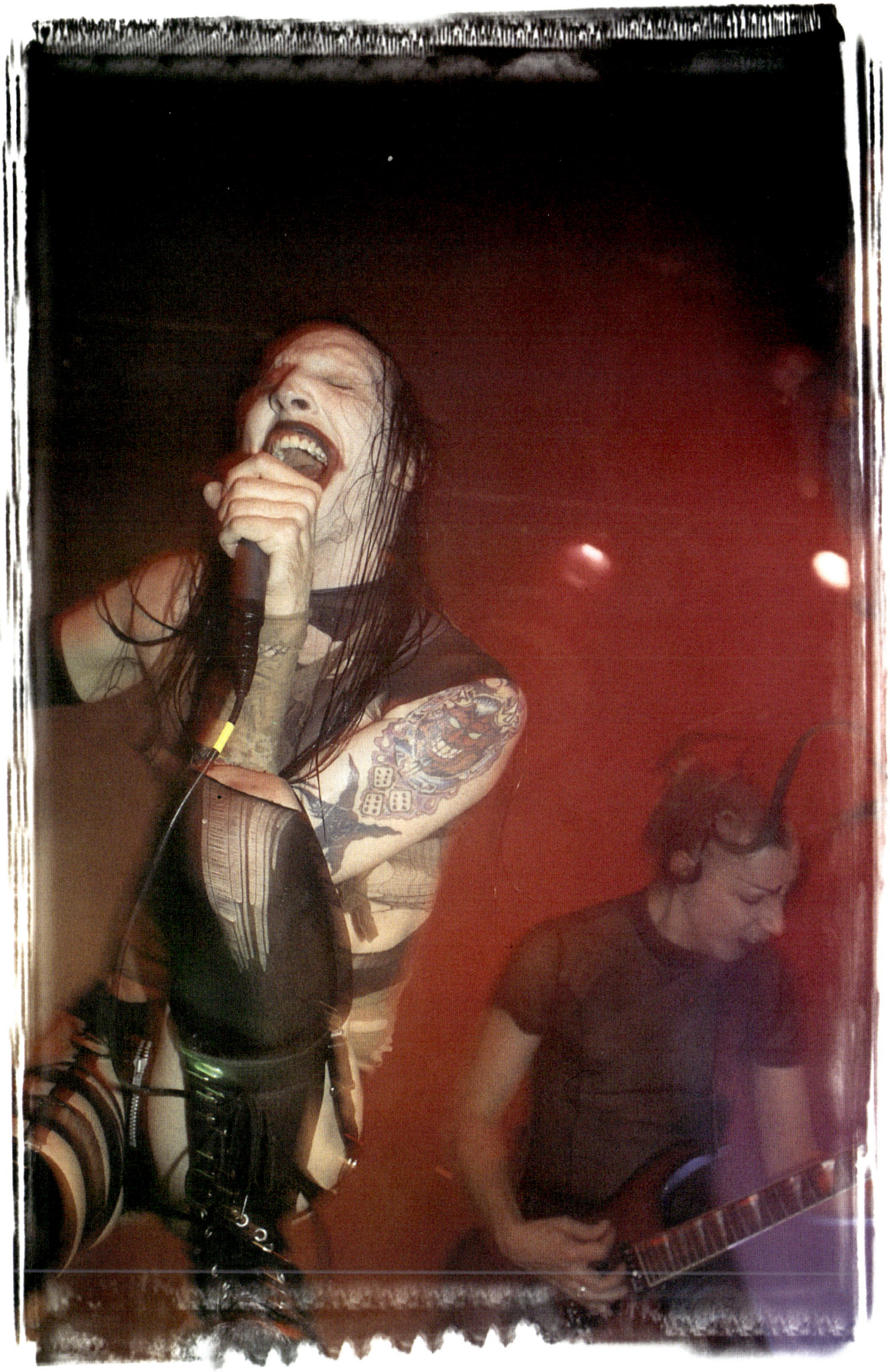

# MARILYN MANSON DISCOGRAPHY

### SINGLES

**Get Your Gunn**
Get Your Gunn / Misery Machine / Mother Inferior Got Her Gunn / Revelation #9
Nothing/Interscope
90902, 1994

**Lunchbox**
Lunchbox / Next Motherf***** (Remix) / Down in the Park / Brown Bag (Remix) / Metal (Remix) / Lunchbox (High School Drop-outs)
Nothing/Interscope
95806, 1994

**Sweet Dreams**
Sweet Dreams / Dance of the Dope Hats (remix) / Down in the Park / Lunchbox (Next Motherfucker)
Australia: MCS/Interscope
IND 95504, 1996

**The Beautiful People**
The Beautiful People
Nothing/Interscope
IND 95514, 1997

### ALBUMS

**Portrait of an American Family**
Prelude (The Family Trip) / Cake and Sodomy / Lunchbox / Organ Grinder / Cyclops / Dope Hat / Get Your Gunn / Wrapped in Plastic / Dogma / Sweet Tooth / Snake Eyes and Sissies / My Monkey / Misery Machine
Nothing/Interscope
INTD-92344, 1994

**Smells Like Children**
The Hands of Small Children / Diary of a Dope Fiend / S****y Chicken Gang Bang / Kiddie Grinder (Remix) / Sympathy for the Parents / Sweet Dreams (Are Made of This) / Everlasting C***sucker (Remix) / F*** Frankie / I Put a Spell On You / May Cause Discoloration of the Urine or Feces / Scabs, Guns and Peanut Butter / Dance of the Dope Hats (Remix) / White Trash (Remixed by Tony F. Wiggins) / Dancing with the One-Legged... / Rock 'n' Roll Nigger
Nothing/Interscope
INTD-92641, 1995

**Antichrist Superstar**
Cycle I - The Heirophant: Irresponsible Hate Anthem / The Beautiful People / Dried Up, Tied and Dead to the World / Tourniquet

Cycle II - Inauguration of the Worm: Little Horn / Cryptorchid / Deformography / Wormboy / Mister Superstar / Angel with the Scabbed Wings / Kinderfeld

Cycle III - Disintegrator Rising: Antichrist Superstar / 1996 / Minute of Decay / The Reflecting God / Man That You Fear
Nothing/Interscope
INTD-90086, 1996

### VIDEOS

Get Your Gunn
Lunchbox
Dope Hat
Sweet Dreams
  (Are Made of This)
The Beautiful People
Tourniquet
Man That You Fear

### EARLY CASSETTE RELEASES

(Titles and track listings unverified):

**Big Black Bus**
White Knuckles / My Monkey / Strange Same Dogma / Red In My Head

**Grist-O-Line**
Dune buggy / Cake and Sodomy / Meat for a Queen / She's Not My Girlfriend

**Lunchbox**
Dune Buggy / My Monkey / Learning to Swim / Cake and Sodomy

**After School Special**
Negative 3 / Lunchbox / Choklit Factory / Cyclops

**The Family Jams**
Dope Hat / Strange Same Dogma / Let Your Ego Die / Thingmaker / White Knuckles / Luci in the Sky with Demons

**Refrigerator**
Cake and Sodomy / Suicide Snowman / My Monkey / Lunchbox / Thrift / Wrapped in Plastic / Dope Hat

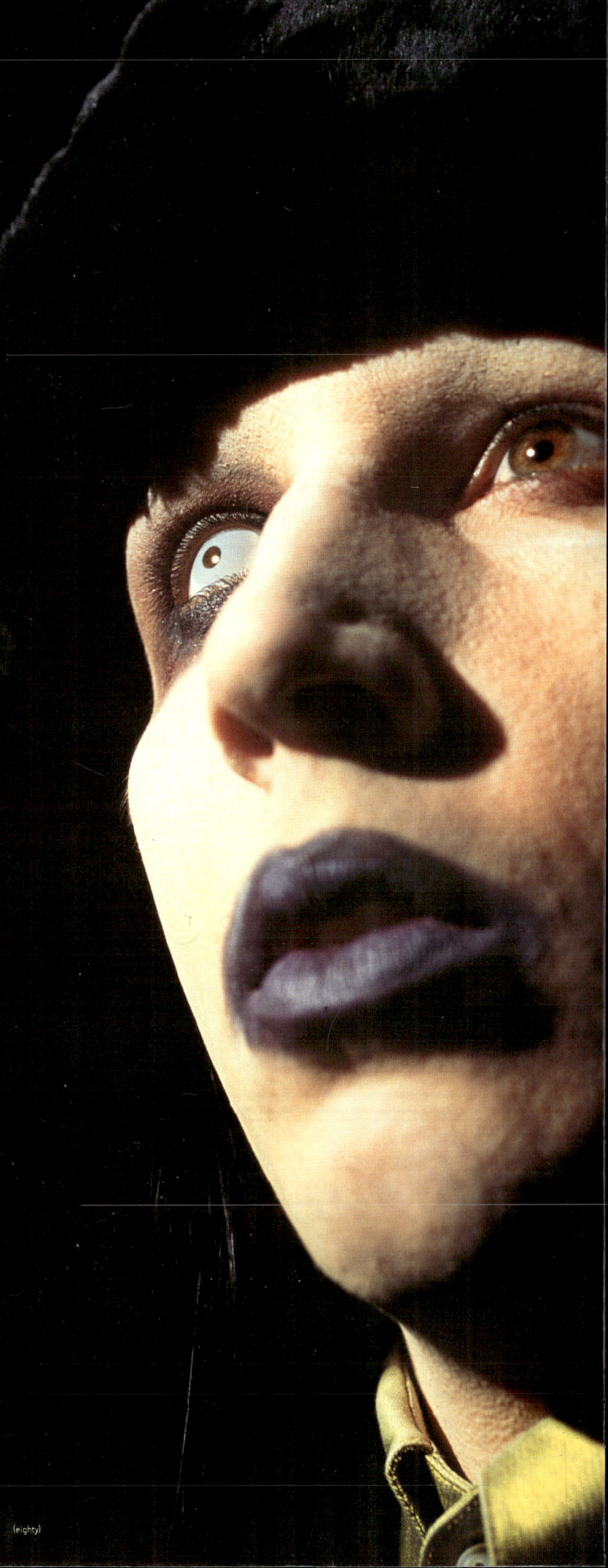